My Royal SWAG
Season 1

Queen Jocelyn
9-4-14

"Viewing Life in
High Definition"

"Supporting another individual's dream is genuine when we do it even before our own dreams become a full reality."

" Merv Mattair"

My Royal Swag: Viewing life in HD
Copyright © 2014 by Marvin Terrell Mattair

All rights reserved. No part of this book may be reproduced in any form without the expressed written permission of the author or publisher except by a reviewer.

Published by:
R.O.Y.A.L.T.Y N/O, INC.
P. O. Box 98
Madison, FL 32341
www.kingsqueens.org
mervmattair@gmail.com

Renewing.Our.Youth's.Actions.Language.Thinking & Yearning to succeed!!

ISBN-10: 0615939090

ISBN-13: 978-0-615-93909-4

LCCN: 2014901560

Cover photograph courtesy of: Istockphoto.com & madisonmediagroup.org

Editors: Cindy Vees and Edna Turner

Cover Creation by: Diane Bass, diane.bass.design@gmail.com

This book is a work of nonfiction. In this book, you have thirty one reality channels that are uncut and viewable only in High Definition. The content is not intended to tear down, but build up and empower the mind of the reader. Read a channel a day, or flip through at your own pace, because you have the remote!! This book is written for ages 13 and up---Peace & Ubuntu, Merv

Table of Contents

Introduction/Intentions

[4]

Introduction/Intentions

Welcome to Season One of *My Royal Swag: Viewing Life in HD*. I am excited that you have decided to wrap your hands around this wonderful product that is guaranteed to bless you in more ways than one. Can you remember watching TV in black and white or on a fuzzy channel back in the day? How does it feel to now have high definition on every channel and on most media devices? With high definition, I am able to see every little detail, so I will never go back to the way it used to be. I took that concept and built off of it, because after various interviews, a great deal of people still view their life in fuzzy black and white and are not able to understand what's going on within the different channels of their life. Things can happen on this journey and because we don't see clearly, we are overlooked, deceived, or left behind. Having a royal swag clearly means that you have the power to make your own decisions and be who you desire to be without being persuaded by society. Who are you? Who are you living for? What's your purpose? Where are you heading? Why do you do what you do? What do you want to be? See, society has answered those questions for us for so long by the use of things that makes us feel comfortable and normal, but it's time to unleash your royal swag and become the person that you desire to be. I have heard rappers being criticized for saying "do what thy wilt," because people associated it with being evil. I don't know why they say it, but I love Jehovah and I believe people should be doing what they desire to do, and get out of the good ole American system that's geared to keep the rich getting richer and the poor getting poorer. As long as you are led by our heavenly Father's Word, it is your right to get out of this box and live your life how you desire. As you flip through the channels of this book, you will see that all of them are in HD and none are in fuzzy black and white. I no longer desire to write like others, so I am using my freestyle writing approach to give you something different on each channel you visit just like watching TV or listening to a CD. I desire to empower our youth, families, willing adults, and all marriages through this masterpiece. My biggest goal is to get more men to read, so I made it fun, educational, and personal. Sometimes, we don't understand what a writer is trying to say, so I included some blue collar parables to insure that the message is clear. I took the every day issues of people, and broke them down in attempt to resonate with the reader. This masterpiece will motivate, empower, inspire, and convict you. After reading this, you will no longer place blame. Don't hold back any longer with your goals and dreams due to people, because from experience, I can tell you that they are going to talk whether you do or you don't. It is your time to live, so grab your mental remote and flip through these channels in search of your spark to acquiring your Royal Swag---Peace & Ubuntu, Merv

Channel 1

Me VS. Me
"My internal hater"

The more that I said to myself "I know I can," there would be a small voice saying "No, I can't," and for so long, I listened to that little voice. I had always prayed to be a speaker and writer and I was willing to do all that I could to make that dream come true, but every time that I got a chance to speak, that voice would be saying things like, "You know you're going to stutter and stumble," "You know these people don't care about what you're talking about", "You know you have to have a college degree to get them to listen, so don't waste your time," or "You know you're going to forget your message," so I went on the scene already defeated and beat up. I still managed to complete the task at hand, but I knew that something was trying to hold me back; I just could not put my hand on it, so it was easy to put it on the white man, the system, non supportive family members, or the black folk mentality, etc. I really found out who my greatest hater was when I was about to step into the professional world of motivational speaking. I had been speaking for no financial charge at churches, juvenile camps, and community events for several years, and people would always speak highly of my messages. The day came for me to elevate my professionalism and speaking to the next level. I was attending a meeting one day and two gentlemen from an abstinence organization called Live The life held a conversation with me. I took pride in my literature, gave them one copy to read and guaranteed that they would love it. The next week I received a phone call from one of the gentlemen asking to purchase 100 of my books to give out during their pep rallies at the various schools they provide their services to. I was proud of myself for utilizing the checkers approach of giving up something in order to get what was needed to reach my goals, but the next conversation was what exposed it all, when I was asked to speak at one of their upcoming pep rallies. I had some butterflies about doing it, but I agreed to speak and then he hit me with the big question, "How much do you charge?" That voice immediately hit me with all the reasons why I was not good enough to get paid and only worth a donation of small amounts, so I told him that I would email him the following day and he agreed. In the meantime, I went through asking several people in my circle about the price that I should charge to speak for forty-five minutes in a professional environment, and the first price I got from someone was $50. All the others were in that range, but Mrs. Edna Turner made it clear that I was called to do what I do, so I needed to charge no less than $250. I thought, "Man that is too much, I am from Madison, I do not have a big time degree, and I don't want to over charge and push them away," but she made it clear that it was time to get paid for what I was worth and not for what people desired to pay me. I prayed about it and decided to email that price to them about 4 a.m. that morning. Of course waiting for their response was like waiting for an AIDS test. I was anxious and afraid at the same time. The reply finally came, but they did not say anything about agreeing with the price. All they mentioned was being in town for another meeting and wanted to meet me at McDonalds shortly after. I immediately started to sweat and think of all the negative reasons as to why they wanted to meet with me, the biggest one being that they had decided to go with someone else because I was rookie status. As I sat there and looked through the glass windows of McDonalds I saw the two gentlemen get out of their vehicle and walk inside as if they were in slow motion. We shook hands, and one of the men started telling me about their religious restrictions based on a grant, how the pep rallies were structured, what to look for in the youth, and that they would have my check the day of the event. I was amazed and excited, but it did not last long, because I started telling myself that they might not pay me like they promised. The day of the event came and I had a whole gym of teenagers to myself and I went harder than ever before. I owned the crowd, the impact was made, the excitement was high, and I walked off that court feeling like a true champion, to only have the gentleman extend his hand with a check in it. That was the day I found out that it was never any of the above obstacles that was holding me back, but it was me

[11]

holding me back. Those men called me back a week later because the speaker they had lined up for another event could not make it, and wanted to know if I could step in for her. The guy told me that they and the kids really enjoyed me and since they were setting up their schedule for the next fiscal year, asked if I would commit to speaking and doing book signings at all their schools. I boldly said "YES." Since I had put the inner me in check, I clearly told the guy that I would need to lock all of the future engagements in at $500 each and he did not hesitate to agree. I can boldly tell you that if you want to slay a giant, start with yourself because that's your greatest road block, your greatest hater, and your worst enemy. When I heard the saying "Keep your enemies close," I was cautious about the outside people, not even knowing that no enemy was closer than the one inside of me. This chapter has nothing to do with bragging about money, but all to do with training your inner self so that you can go harder than ever before at accomplishing your goals and dreams. So many of us have been trained from birth to blame others for reasons as to why we can't get to the next level, but I am here to remove that lie. Yes, people will always try to hold you down, but they can only go as far as you will allow them to. They do not know you like your inner hater does and to be honest, when people try to hold you back, it has nothing to do with you, but everything to do with them and the personal struggles they are faced with. You can toss their smelly contributions to your misery in the trash quickly and when they don't see their garbage stinking up your life, they will try placing it in someone else's.

Being from a small town can easily cause a person to think small and then have their small thinking validated by other people who think just like that. Although small thinking is not getting you on another level, it's at least normal to the people that you are around the most and because it's normal, then it makes you comfortable. The problem is you never grow to your fullest potential. As soon as you attempt to go against the grain, your greatest hater, if not tamed, will be the first to give you all the reasons to remain where you are, attracting others who feel the same way, because a miserable inner you has to have company to keep you from taking that leap of faith. People in small towns are often accustomed to small thoughts, so earning $50 in their eyes should have taken about three hours to make. If you are still suffering in dealing with the inner you, then you need to be mindful of who you get advice from, because you may start going backwards with wrong counsel. You will easily begin to blame those people and your surroundings for your lack of success, when all along it was you that was afraid to fail, afraid to make changes, afraid to be criticized, afraid to be laughed at, afraid to be in charge, and afraid to manage the great results of your efforts. When your inner you is tamed to work for you, you will begin to do the unimaginable and soon begin to attract people who will think just like you or better. The small thinkers will either be

[13]

motivated by you to check themselves or they will depart from you. If you are walking in fear and doubt, then you need to have a conversation with yourself because that is not healthy.

You need to be mindful of what you're listening to and what you're watching, realizing that those are sources of enter-tain-ment (detained, so that something can enter inside of you), are geared towards making you think and feel some kind of way. You should take advantage of a 32 Day Royal Swag Challenge of doing something different, consistently for 31 days and using the 32nd day as gravy, making a statement to the inner you that you are determined to go beyond what's expected. Those 31 days represents the mash potatoes, but you only get the gravy when you do a little extra. Who want to eat mash without the gravy? When you push yourself enough, your inner you will refuse to have mash without gravy, so each time you exceed that finish line of success, you may hear your inner you saying "Now that's gravy baby." Here are a few foods that strengthen an untamed inner you: daily gossip, constantly watching and listening to negativity through media sources, complaining and listening to others complain constantly, being in an idle state of mind too often, making excuses why something can't happen, hanging around doubtful people all the time, having a negative attitude, and desiring to live in drama day in and day out. I am so confident now and I refuse to look back. I have made my greatest hater my footstool to the point that my inner ME works for me now, telling me positive affirmations

[14]

daily such as, "I am the best," "I can do anything," "I have that Midas touch," "I wont give up," "I have standards," and many more. Talking to yourself is not something that is welcomed in society, because people will think you're crazy. I happen to think you're crazy if you don't talk to yourself. If you want it, then get it. If you have a dream, make it a reality. If you want to live a fearless life, then you have the right to that. Your body is your house and it's time to get your house in order from the inside out. Today, it's no longer Me VS. Me, but Us VS. The World, and together there is nothing that me and my inner me can't accomplish. Your Royal Swag has been unleashed, so get on your grind and refuse to waste anymore of your precious time---Peace & Ubuntu, Merv

Channel 2

I Said "I Do" To Another Man!!
"Don't judge me"

Yes, my name is Merv, I have let the cat out of the bag, and I am proud about it. People can say what they want to say about me, but I love this Man. I can remember the day when I proposed to my girlfriend, I had no real clue about what was expected of me as a husband, so I started to pay more attention to my dad and other men to try and get it down to a science. It was hard because I could only see so far into their lives and I needed to see and witness more. I was seeing on television and around my community how men were losing their families because of infidelity, causing their kids to suffer the worst end of the deal and I wanted no part of that. I wanted something that was going to last, but I did not trust my own intentions. I had questions about trusting myself when I was out of town and from around my future wife. I struggled with respecting her wishes unless she was right there in my presence. That was so called normal for a man. If I was able to make her feel and look good while around her, but able to get loose with the homeboys when I was not in her presence, I was good. Well, I wanted no part of that either, given the fact that I had a little daughter to role model for. I was a lost brotha with good intentions but not enough examples to make me believe that a marriage could not just last, but be productive and healthy.

I started to pray and read my Word often and the more I read the clearer things began to seem for me. I found out through my reading that I did not really have a conscience and that was scary, but that explained why I was able to do doggish things behind someone's back without having any remorse. I kept reading and reading, until I realized that I was getting ready to say "I do" and marry the wrong person. All along I had my eyes on that gorgeous lady, but my heart was with and on another Man. Never in a million years did I think that I would be saying that I found the Man of my life that would make all of my dreams come true. I had to make some changes in my life to make sure that this Man was first in everything thing that I did. I learned more about Him, especially the fact that He is real jealous. I had done enough reading and I was ready to make this big move in my life so that I could truly live a productive life.

My wedding day came around and like I mentioned in my first book "*Word to My King & Queens,*" I was ready to exceed the traditional wedding vows. I did not have to move to another state or get government permission to marry this Man, the choice was all mine. We went through with the ceremony and now I am able to look back to see what my prior issues were before saying "I do." I don't have the same issues that I had prior to getting married, because that Man who I said "I do" to is always there with me and always seems to catch me before I fall. Although I stood at the altar and held hands with my wife, I said "I do" to God because as long as I keep pleasing Him at the forefront, my wife is well taken care of. I still received a test of my faithfulness even after saying "I do," but I have a conscience now that serves as my first consequence, so I am able to stop, think, and act. This thing is real and if we don't grab hold to our Father's hand, we will continue to lose families and marriages, which will in return influence the future family structure of our children, causing dysfunction. Saying "I do" to another Man has made my mind stronger, my love deeper, my joy greater, and my visions and dreams clearer. Whatever it takes to keep your marriage and family together, take advantage of it before losing out on the benefits of that unity. When any man decides to say "I do" to our heavenly Father, he is setting his family up for a healthy future and they will forever thank him for doing so. I know that some people try to do it on their own, but I am a witness that there is no way of doing this thing on your own because it's too heavy. It's so heavy that it takes two men to carry and if it's those late night break downs about the bills not being able to be paid, "He got you," and if it's the heavy burden of having your home in foreclosure status, etc., He will help you carry that weight and He won't leave you. If you're having marital problems, He will keep you from falling and if you just don't have the answer, He is right there waiting to be asked the question. I know that if you're a man reading this and you did not have your earthly father in your life to depend on, that you're probably feeling some type of way about this, but I encourage you to not let what your earthly father did not do, keep you from experiencing what your heavenly Father is ready, able, and willing to do for you. They can call me weak, but I need that Man and I cannot go anywhere without Him. I was trying to get my first two books purchased by a company, but they said that they could not purchase them because I mentioned God inside of them. I must be crazy because I am mentioning Him again in this one and I refuse to be ashamed of or disown Him just to get some earthly success. When I said "I do," I really meant that and my life has been a blessing, even in the midst of my trials. Ladies, when you are looking that man in the eyes at the altar, make sure that your "I do" is to God. That way, you won't take many of your man's mistakes personal, but you will understand that he is human and as long as you stay true to what you promise, God will take care of him. As soon as you lose focus and try to fix things yourself, that's when it all starts to go downhill. If your marriage is going south and you can't seem to figure it out on your own, maybe you two need to get together on your own and redo your vows, but next time, say "I do" to your heavenly Father. Don't worry about the crowd of people, because He says in His Word that "if two or three come together for His name sake that He will be in the midst," Matthew 18:20.

So many of us try to go around the Biblical principles when it comes to having a successful and peaceful marriage to only cause chaos, when all we have to do is follow the scripture that's already written. I feel that oftentimes in these days at the altar people are saying "I do" to sex, and that causes more confusion than anything. What if right now sex was eradicated from all marriages, would any of us be equipped to still make our partners happy? Would the providing that the Word says for a man to do replace that loss and keep that woman feeling like a woman or would she seek out another because she was being provided for and loved through sex? Would the submissiveness that the Word says for women to practice replace that loss and keep that man feeling like a king, or would he seek for another because the woman pleased him with sex while he overlooked her contentious ways? Without sex, so many of us would be exposed, because sex is a tool that can confuse a person with happiness and hide many flaws. If the only way you can make your spouse feel like a king or a queen is through sex, then you need to go back and say "I do" to the right person and let His Word guide your marriage and no longer yourselves. That's real talk. Don't waste anymore time playing around with your marriage because the longer you keep Him out of it, the devil will continue to keep the confusion at the forefront. Today is the day that you both hold hands and say "I do" to another Man.---Peace & Ubuntu, Merv

[20]

Channel 3

Yesterday's Success, is Today's Competition
"Self motivation is the best motivation"

We have all had some sort of success in our lives that we are proud of, even if it was minor. I am here to tell you that if we don't utilize that success as a hurdle to jump over or as competition to defeat, it will eventually turn into complacency, especially if the cheers are still in the background. Each day brings about another opportunity to become better at something in our lives. Often times in America, the ones who don't have the businesses, the millions of dollars, the movie star status or the popularity, don't really work at making themselves better, but rather are making the ones who are already successful more successful. We have one life to live, so I say if you got an A on a test yesterday, then today you should be trying to get an A+ if you are able to. If you scored a sixty yard touchdown yesterday, although the media and fans are celebrating the new school record, you should be practicing harder today to score at least a sixty-one yard touchdown next game. If you wrote your first book and people celebrated your fine work up until this day, it needs to be made known to them that they have not read anything until they read your next one. It's time to get in the game

[21]

and go hard for you, so stick out your chest a little bit and get on your grind! If you know that you suffer with a bad attitude and yesterday you were able to respect one person, then today, you should be striving for two people to respect. Absent fathers, if you finally came through for your kids by taking them to the park yesterday, although the mom is happy and the community people who saw you are patting you on the back, do not get wrapped up in all the hype, but instead, next time take them to a theme park! Today is the day where we no longer let our success of yesterday interrupt our greater success of today.

No longer let another day of your life pass by without doing inventory on what you have to do better tomorrow. If you have been in a tough environment that doesn't promote, support, or encourage you bettering yourself, then today you should be at least one inch closer to getting out of it. It hurts to see so much talent buried alive, so I tell you that if the day ever comes that you refuse to push yourself to the next level, this world will go ahead and toss dirt on you and allow you to walk around dead because dead walking people are dollar signs to America. If you are a pastor that preached a sermon yesterday that brought one person to the love of Christ, then today you should go just that much harder with the goal of bringing in two or more. If you are a wife that struggles with contentious ways, but yesterday you were able to give your husband the respect he needed during a situation making him feel like a man, then today, you should go even harder and make him feel like a king. If you are a husband that suffers with infidelity, but yesterday you told your mistress NO, then today, you should be working on erasing her number out your phone. If you are a lady who knows that you're gaining too much weight, and you walked a half a mile yesterday, then today you should be doing one mile. Self motivation is the best motivation and in order to get the results you want, yesterday's success has to be today's competition. Success is measured differently with the use of our own personal rulers, so making a million dollars, etc., may not be in your success plan, but daily growth has to be. I don't care who you are, you are guaranteed one thing in this life and that's the fact that you will one day pass away regardless of anything. Drake says it best in one of his songs "Everybody dies, but not everybody lives!!!" Don't worry about challenging someone else when you cannot conquer self. That would be like saying that you have the power to deal with the major worldly temptations that the devil brings your way but you cannot even stop eating honey buns on a regular basis. Start with the small stuff first. If you are a hustler and you landed a contract yesterday with an organization to wash their cars, then today, you should be more confident in knowing that since you had your game on point to land that, you should chalk that one up and today start work on getting a major corporation checked off on your board. Our greatest mental advancement in this life will come from challenging our successes from yesterday and not getting caught up in old hand claps. You are great today and even greater by tomorrow, so knock off that dirt and start to live instead of just waiting to die. When the day comes that you can conquer self, then you will be able to have some "away games," where you successfully compete against others for the prize. When that day comes, I will encourage you to rise early on them, because the early bird catches the worm. Don't waist time lying around idle as if something is going to fall in your lap. While they're sleeping, you're up praying and doing a little more than what you did yesterday and refusing to cheat yourself. If you are an athlete, you should be up jumping rope to the rhythm of their snoring. That new job is yours, that championship game is yours, that A school grade is yours, that big contract is yours, that new business needs you as CEO, that speaking engagement belongs to you, that grant is coming your way, and if there is anything else you want, as long as you can believe it, speak it, pursue it boldly, then you can claim it. Yesterday is dead, today is dying and tomorrow is ready for whatever you bring into it, so unleash your Royal Swag and prepare for victory! ~ Let's Go!!!!!!!---Peace & Ubuntu, Merv

Channel 4

The Family Tree
"With broken branches"

I have heard, read, and written on several occasions about this thing called family, and how important it is for the growth of an individual. Family is a group of people who you can depend on to give love to you when no one else will love you. Family is a group of people who will support all that you do even when no one else will support you. Family is a group of people who will be in your corner when you make dumb decisions because they believe that you can bounce back. When family shows up for you, it sends a feeling on the inside that can't be explained. Family is where most of us pick up certain habits and learn certain wives-tales that we take into our own marriages and teach to our own children. Family was meant to be a great thing and I will dare that it is, and if it's not, it can be.

A family tree is what we call it when we can go way back to where we think our blood line started all the way up to the last baby born. The family tree consists of grandparents and great ones, mom, dad, aunts, uncles, cousins, brothers, sisters, nieces, nephews and more. The tree begins to grow branches of a family, who built their own identity because some of the traditions they grew up with were not beneficial to keep practicing. Each branch on a tree is just a little different, and that's what makes the tree unique. When everyone comes together, you never know what to expect, but a good time is guaranteed. I have seen some family trees that have some strong branches, and I have seen some that have some weak or broken branches. I have to admit that the strong winds and the toxic watering of this world's evilness have weakened the branches on several family trees and now that I view life in high definition, I can see it clearly. The only way that a family tree can remain strong is if it is watered with love, understanding, relationships, peace, empathy, support, etc. It does not cost anything for those items and we will never run out, so every tree should be strong. The truth is we have become a selfish nation that has placed a bad stamp on the word family.

The family tree with broken branches has become the norm in America and it is considered acceptable. Don't take anything personal if your family tree has broken branches as long as you're watering it with the proper things often. There are some things you can't expect to receive from a family tree with broken branches that you would receive automatically from a family tree with strong sturdy branches. If you desire to be respected for your beliefs, you're only going to be talked about. If you desire to be loved, you're only going to be treated OK in their presence with their smiles, hugs, and jokes as a front. If you want to be supported, you will receive nothing at all or their bare minimum just to say they supported you. If you need to borrow money, they will give you the run around to only tell you no, just to see you fall. If you have a business, they will never mention it and hope that you never talk about it because it hurts them to hear anything successful about it. If you have a great idea, they will knock it when it comes out of your mouth and praise it when it comes out of another's mouth as their idea. If you are celebrating a successful moment, they will give an excuse to not come, but when you're dead and gone, the church won't be able to hold them all for the funeral. When your kids get into trouble, instead of them coming through for support, they talk about them to others. When you see and hear them in church proclaiming to love God, it makes you wonder if they are telling the truth because they can't see God to be so much in love with Him but suffer with loving someone they see often.

Broken families are everywhere, so many people join churches and gangs to get that which they are not receiving from their blood family and that's ridiculous. I want to say to the people who are watering their family tree with toxic stuff to please stop today because you are only making it harder for generations to come. Strong family is the key to many people's success and if you can just stop hating for a little while to think, you will see that in the end, the entire family is successful when at least one makes it out. So many families have so much talent, but because it's a family tree with broken branches, oftentimes the family would rather live a life of barely making it, just to keep the talent from being revealed to others, especially if the hater is content with where they are currently. My motto is "supporting another individual's dream is genuine when we do it even before our own dreams become a full reality," and I try to practice that daily. Even though I have a fairly supportive family, maybe my actions might just encourage others to do better. If you are part of a family with broken branches, I encourage you to water it daily with love through your actions. Hopefully the broken branches will begin to thicken back up and then contribute to the beauty of the family tree. If you are the broken branch and wonder why people don't come around you much or refuse to come to a family event while you're there, maybe they have common sense to know that it is not wise to stand by a broken branch because it could fall at anytime. The strength of a family tree rests in the actions of the people, so let's all go hard to build stronger branches that are able to hold the next generation of youth on.---Peace & Ubuntu, Merv

Channel 5

One Church, Can Make One Man, Despise All Churches!!
"The truth shall cometh out"

I have heard so many people place blame on the church as to why they don't go anymore, so I had to investigate it for myself. I had to pick something up from a church one evening while no one was there, so I decided while there to take a seat in the congregation seats and look into the pulpit. I stayed there for a little while just to see if the church building was going to make me feel uncomfortable, unworthy, not wanted, etc. For some reason, that building did not restrict my prayers, it did nothing but allow me a place of safety to worship without any outside distractions from the world. As a self seeking myth buster, I declare that a church building does not cause a person to not attend church services anymore.

I drove to my home one day and just sat in the drive way thinking deeply about this topic while my family was out doing normal weekday things. On the outside looking in I realized that this is only a house, but my family on the inside of it makes it a home, so then I began to research more about buildings. Today, people all over have made any abandoned building their church or place of worship, such as old store buildings, old clubs, hotels, and portions of abandoned schools. Let's take the old club building that's now a church building. The building has never been reconstructed, the only two changes is the removal of the naked lady on the sign outside and replaced with a cross, as well as the changing of the locks on the doors, and so I ask, what really made the building become a church? The church is supposed to be accessible to people at anytime, but I had to use a key to get in that one, so the more I think about it, the building is not what people are talking about.

That empty church and that empty house are only buildings until the people come in and make it what it is. People with the mind to drink, party, dance, and throw a few hay makers, cause a particular building to become a club, and people who come to worship and praise God cause a particular building to become a church sanctuary. The people are the real churches, and people are the ones driving other believers out of the church building. If the people going to a club at night did not go there to do the normal club stuff, people would not go to that club anymore. Let me help you understand this more. Say we have the first ten people in "Club Get It In" already getting things jumping off before you arrive. Now you already know that it's been a long week and you're going to turn up no matter what, so you need to get there early. You step in and you see a few people reading Bibles, a couple people playing checkers, one couple on the dance floor dancing, and the DJ playing Shirley Caesar. Although you were early, you probably won't try to hang around to see what else is coming in. You leave and enter another building called "Club Mannish" and you begin to smile because you see all the goodies that are expected. After going back to Club Mannish for a year, you know what to expect and you always get it, so you never return to Club Get It In ever again. That doesn't have anything to do with the building, but all to do with the intentions of the people inside of the building. People have been called church hoppers, unbelievers, and much more for leaving a church building to attend another because the intentions of the people inside did not portray the love of God. I have witnessed people suffer several years in a church building with other people, because it's family and grandma and nem said to stay at your home church until you die, even if it's you, the pastor, one deacon and two choir members. People shop at the same grocery store for years because they know what they are going to get when they get there, but when you attend some church buildings, often times you don't. It begins to tamper with your spiritual life causing a person to go looking for the wrong things, such as what someone has on, how many people attend, who is begging for money, and the next piece of juicy Sunday evening gossip. Yes, some church people have created three services, the Sunday school in the morning, worship service at noon, and Sunday evening gossip. If believers are the church, then it has to be said that our evil intentions and motives have

[31]

caused several people to despise other believers as well as the buildings that believers dwell in. It's alright for someone to switch insurance companies because of crooked people, but if you switch churches because of the people, you're looked down upon for having no faith. The guys under the tree with their beer in their hands watching everyone enter and exit the church buildings can perhaps point to over half of those people who have intentionally misrepresented the true love of Christ. The guys under the tree make it clear that one church has made one man despise all churches. Whoever approaches them with a Bible verse, they may ask them to walk it out, not read it out. The man under the tree will tell you that he doesn't hold a Bible in his hands, but he reads your Bible every day through your supposed spiritual actions. He makes it clear that we can't talk love and then display hate, because we are only turning people away from getting their lives right. We are open twenty four hours a day and others should know that they can come to us when they are in need of something and it does not matter their color. The true church is not open for only a certain race of people, but because the sanctuary houses that perception, we begin to walk in it. We don't have locks on us and we can come to you instead of you coming to us. We, the real church will serve you in the open, not only behind the walls of a building. I remember hearing about a man running for office. Some spiritual people of different race approached him and stated that they really want him to win and that they were going to support him, but they couldn't put his signs in their yards because of what their race of people would say or think.

I have heard pastors preach about us being the real church and I commend them for doing that. Those pastors are expecting people to come into a church building with high expectations, full of love, and much more. They know that someone has been going through a rough time, being beat up in the world all week and the last thing they need is to come into a church building around church people that have unbiblical motives. I know that some people are going to find this controversial, but in order for people to know, it has to be put out there. No, it is not normal for a church building with church people in it to not prosper in every area and not give folks the love, peace, truth, structure, and stability that our Father expects. God is not the author of confusion, but man is, so if you are ever confused as to whether you're in a church building or somewhere less than where God would have you, based on the actions of the people there, the chances of you prospering there is not likely. That human church that has made you despise all other churches may be a fake worshipper. Pray for discernment and please give it another chance on finding the truth before this world pulls you in and traps you. We as a people are very quick to point out a dead beat father, a racist, a drug addict, a hooker, a crook, and a liar, but if you call out a fake Christian, you are now judging and God does not want that.

[33]

During meetings and other daily conversations with people, I often hear and have said myself that the churches do not get involved enough and we would name them one by one. That was before I viewed this life in high definition. Now I see that we cannot expect the same people who refuse to love, get along, and support others Monday through Saturday, to all of a sudden when they have on a suit or a dress, feel any different about you on Sunday. We see so many communities falling by the wayside with hardly anyone in the streets doing good deeds during the week, but "Early Sunday Morning," the church vans hit the streets and churches are entering into the sanctuaries making joyful sounds. I imagine a community with no church buildings, but a lot of churches, building each other up with a strong foundation to be able to withstand the pressures of this world. Some church buildings have caused the real churches to become wall to wall servers, in my circle servers, is it going to benefit my building servers, and worship with my own race of people servers. When a homeowner is required to pay monthly mortgage in order to keep his home, he takes pride in that home and refuses to let anything happen to it. I tend to believe that when some people tithes for so long, they forget why they are doing it and begin to view it as a required mortgage, that causes them to fall deeply in love with that building and not in love with God. If a true church loves God, then we will not have to wait to get to our sanctuary on Sundays to show it.

[34]

I will go on the record to say that having so many church buildings has caused more division amongst the people, more so than the civil rights era did. I want to encourage everyone to form a relationship with our heavenly Father because that is the most important. Even in challenging times, we still have some pastors that refuse to let their people be deceived, so they try their best to lead by example. I give this personal "My Small Town Hero" shout out, to a young, thirty-four year old pastor, father, husband, and community leader, Minister Marcus Hawkins, Sr. of Madison, Florida, and Pastor of Shiloh Missionary Baptist Church. There are many more that I can brag on from my city, because they are indeed going hard for the right reasons. If you see a pastor in your city who is trying to do it right, please stop and congratulate him, because oftentimes, the people feed off the vibes of their pastor. To all the awesome believers across this world who are putting in the true work, let us continue to stay on the grind for our heavenly Father and be the church that draws others in and not one that turns them away. Let's have Church.--- Peace & Ubuntu, Merv

Channel 6

My Dreads Locked Doors
"I cut the locks, & the doors came open"

I have to admit that I proudly rocked my dreadlocks for twelve years with a smile, but often a frown on my face. I am not sure as to why I would frown up so much when I was pleased with my appearance. I remember when I was first growing them and they were stuck to my head, they would give me little extra piece of motivation for some reason. When they started to get some swing to them when I would turn my head, I became the man. I would often just turn around to look at someone real quick just to show off the swing action of those pretty locks. I had my personal hair dresser doing them because I wanted the best looking locks around, but the longer they got, the more expensive they got, so I had to turn to my wife to help me. Yes, my wife started doing them for me once a month and she made them look extra good. I was able to tie those boys up in a beehive and do all sorts of styles with them, and you did not want me to throw on a pair of glasses and grab a guitar. I remember inquiring about jobs and the first question I would ask is "do I have to cut my hair?" I did not want to go to the military because I refused to cut my hair.

I owned a 66 Chevy Bel-Air that was clean as a whistle. One day, my wife and I were in a different state Christmas shopping and we had the windows down just enjoying the cool breeze. I had my hair down and I guess the connection of the hair and car gave a cop a reason to pull me over. After we stopped, the cop made it clear verbally that I was swerving. He then asked if we could step out because he smelled weed. I replied "Sir, we don't smoke no weed, my wife just opened some potato chips," but he was confident in his nose. This dude pulled my seats out of my car, allowed his dogs to sniff all through my trunk, only to turn and apologize for the mistake. I knew that the hair played a part in that, but that was not enough for me to cut it.

I was working at a juvenile camp as a direct care staff person at the bottom of the ranks, but I desired to go to the top. People would always tell me to cut my hair, but I wanted to prove to everyone that having locked hair on your head does not define you. To me, it was all about the character and swag of the individual wearing it. To keep from going through the entire ladder of success, I will make it clear that I worked my way up the ladder five positions higher in eight years and became the Program Director with long locks. I proved the fact that it was not about the hair, but I had to keep living and learning. I worked as program director for a while and after leaving, I went straight into contracting and speaking. I was able to get those youth to listen to me quick because I thought it was the hair, so I would let it hang when I was in their presence. I was able to get some contracts to perform my talents as well, but not the ones that I knew I needed. I remember not having time to get my hair re-twisted and having a professional community meeting to attend, so I put a hat on to cover up the flaws. When I got there, someone wanted to pray and because I honor my heavenly Father, I had to take off my hat. That was my first time really praying with my eyes open because I was concerned about what the people were going to think and who were looking so that I could explain to them afterwards. It was like everyone was looking for a little while, so I just weathered that storm. After the prayer, I had to put my hat back on a certain way because my hair was so long. Again, people were watching me do that as well. I would have so many people telling me how neat and long my hair was that I only wanted to keep it looking good. When someone told me that I had the best looking dreads in town, I flipped out. Now don't forget, I was a grown man still being motivated by a head full of hair. I got a chance to speak to adults at churches and community events, and even an opportunity to speak at Florida State University, but what I needed seemed to not be there.

I remember traveling to different theme parks with my family and being unable to dive in the pools because my hair would get wet and it took so long for it to dry. Those locks caused me to go twelve years without being able to fully enjoy outings of that nature with my family. I did not worry, because I had them locks baby, and they were looking good. People would still tell me to cut my hair, but I would always think about the number of people telling me how good they looked, so I refused to cut them. I remember being in a store and I had my hair hanging down to my waist. I went up to this little baby and she started crying. The mom immediately said "It's the hair, Merv." "Wow, was that little baby seeing something that I was not?" I thought to myself. I would coach football games and see how some of the parents would look at me when I had to raise my voice at some of the kids, but I was not cutting my hair; I did not care what anyone thought. I was an author, a contractor and a motivational speaker with dreadlocks. I had proven my point to the world, but my heavenly Father wanted me to go a lot further. Some doors were still locked because of people's perceptions no matter how good I was. My wife had just done my hair the week before I did my normal spiritual fast, and my locks were looking good. I was in my man cave doing my spiritual fast from 7 a.m. to 3 p.m. with nothing to eat and praying at the top of every hour. It started out great as always, but the challenge came during the 12 p.m. hour. As I was praying, it came to me clearly that the reason some of those doors were locked was because of my dreads and that I needed to cut them. I immediately called in the house to my wife, told her, and she was all for it. By 3 p.m. I was in Barber Steve Williams chair getting a school boy hair cut.

I had to seriously get adjusted to it and the people around me had to as well, because most of them had only associated me with long hair. We took our kids to a park shortly after cutting them and I was able to swim freely with no restrictions, so I had a ball. There was a little bit of Samson going on because for so long I was thinking that my talent and strength was in my hair. I had to test it when I was asked to speak to a group of youth for the first time after cutting the locks. I was sweating profusely, because every time I spoke in the past, the youth would be fascinated with my locks, but they were no longer there. What were they going to focus on? I carried my message in that room and seemed to have gotten a better response than I ever did, making me realize that it was me, and never my hair. Shortly after that speaking engagement, I went to a meeting, shook a few hands, and landed a nice contract with the University of South Florida to teach Sexual Education classes to youth. Through them, I got my chance to finally be the keynote speaker at the University of Florida during a summer conference for educators. I often look back at my pictures when I had the locks compared to now and I am glad that I was led to cut them.

I am rolling with different opportunities in my life now and I do not have dreadlocks as a distraction anymore. I had to cut the locks in order to get full access to what was behind the doors. It was not because of man telling me to do so, but it was because of a relationship that I had with my heavenly Father. If you are rocking your locks, I will encourage you to rock them with style and professionalism and refuse to cut them just because someone says to, because you will only grow them right back. If you think that power is in your hair, pray about it and do not get so caught up in the hype behind it, or you will cause opportunities slip by you. There is nothing wrong with wearing your locks guys, and yes, you can still accomplish your goals. Just be mindful that having them will cause a great deal of profiling from prospects as well as law enforcement. If you have dreads and you are trying to get certain doors to open in your life, you will probably be doing yourself a favor by cutting them. Don't put your success on hold for a fad bro; go get what is yours while the opportunity still presents itself. Just like loud speakers in the trunk, big shiny rims, and extreme sagging of the pants gets old, so will treasuring locks. Don't neglect opportunities in the midst of a people pleasing mindset that you're going to one day grow out of. People will tell you to cut your hair for several reasons such as, "They see something special underneath them," "They can't grow any hair on their head," "They are offended by your appearance," "They have had bad profiling experiences and want to save you," "They feel that God doesn't want a man wearing long hair," etc. Sincerely, fast and pray, and you should eventually know when it's time. As for me, my season was up. I can say that at some point in your life, the locks not being cut will create limited access to what is behind specific doors. Do you!!--Peace & Ubuntu, Merv

[41]

Channel 7

We Are Saved Not Soft, So Don't Get It Twisted!!
"Getting our 3 Hebrew Boys on"

I try to visualize the three Hebrew boys from the Bible, when they were placed in a situation to give in to the way of the world or stand for what they believed in. There was a great number of people obeying the laws of the land that was established by man, but those three brothers were like "We ain't about to sell out." They were threatened to be tossed in a fiery furnace if they did not bow down like the rest of the people were doing. I can picture those dudes saying to the king and all of his partners that had the others operating out of fear, "We are not sure who you think we serve, but we are saved not soft, homey." Those brothers stood strong and refused to fear a system or a people because they knew who they served. They were tossed in that extra hot furnace while others watched to see them suffer. They, in return, displayed to all of them that even while being in that fire, they still could not be harmed, because they had Jehovah with them. That proved to all those watching that those boys were not as soft as they took them to be. It did not take them passing one blow, but having faith and standing for what they believed in.

[42]

Being a follower of Christ, I know that it gets tough, because people expect you to turn the other cheek after demolishing the other one. People expect you to give them money without expecting it back in return. People expect you to accept them talking to you any kind of way and you not say a word back to them. People expect you to follow every law that they make, because the Bible encourages us to obey the laws of the land. People think that you can't take a firm stand on matters that don't involve church related issues. I see so many Christians being taken advantage of and it is sad. I love Christ a lot, and I will continue to be a servant, but it must be made known that we are saved and not soft, so don't get it twisted.

During a meeting, there was a lady with a real bad attitude, who was ready, able, and willing to take on whomever. No one wanted a piece of her because they were afraid of her response, so she got much respect from everyone inside of that meeting. At the end of the meeting, she got what she wanted, so her mission was accomplished. Another meeting took place where a very respectful Christian woman had some issues, but her approach was very appropriate and professional. The people laughed at her and pretty much told her in their own words to get a life. The lady did not disrespect them; she just took what they delivered and went on about her business.

There was a person who needed to borrow some money to immediately pay a major bill, so he went to the local drug dealer to

[43]

get it. He explained to them that the money needed to be paid back in five days and the borrower agreed. The drug dealer was known around town for hurting people, so after the borrower paid the bill, he made sure that the money was paid back in three days. That same person borrowed money from a follower of Christ and agreed to have it paid back in one week. It was one year later and the borrower had not paid the money back. They would see each other in the store and the borrower would talk to the lender as if he forgot he owed money, so the Christian said, "God, please forgive me of my debts as I have to forgive the debts of this person."

There was a supervisor who had one person on her team who walked the Word and believed in respecting authority. The other employees did not care and if the supervisor ever came off wrong, they would check her. The supervisor would take advantage of the respectful person by making her work the late hours, making her come in for others who she was afraid to question, and it only got worse. I am not sure if you have been through such circumstances, but I am sure you have witnessed it and much more. It's time for us to stand for what's right instead of letting this world drag us like we are not anchored by the Master. The three Hebrew boys did nothing violent, but they were well respected after they stood and said "Enough is enough." We have to be willing to look stupid sometimes because I know that some of the people that were around the Hebrew boys wanted to stand as well, but they were afraid. I can hear them saying "Look at them, they are about to make it bad for all of us," and some of them probably promised to stand with those boys prior to then, but when the King mentioned that furnace, they forgot what they promised and would have probably denied a conversation with them if they were questioned. How many times on a job, the people overall are being treated like slaves and during break time, they all complain, but no one wants to stand? When we take a stand for something that needs to change, just because we are sent to the furnace is not a bad thing, it's just proving to this world that we are saved and not soft, because we have the Master with us.

There are a lot of kids who are bullied because they try to walk the Word and do things the right way. I say stand and say no more and believe that the Master has your back. You aren't suppose to take beatings, because you're saved not soft, so fear no more and know that there is power in the furnace. We will no longer allow those people to take advantage of us just because they feel that we are soft. No, we are not claiming to be hard by any means, but we are far from being a pushover. If you come, you need to come correct because we are no longer afraid of your furnace, and, to be honest, we like the furnace because it gives us a chance to regroup with our Coach. If you borrow money from a follower of Christ, please don't assume that we don't want it back and mistake our kindness for weakness. If we want you to keep it, then that would be discussed up front. You are no longer going to talk to us any kind of way as if we are children. Yes indeed, we are

[45]

saved, but nowhere close to being soft. Our maturity in the Word will give us the words to say to keep you in your pathetic little places. No longer will you take our issues during meetings for granted just because we deliver them to you in a mature manner instead of utilizing violence and threats. No longer will you be successful in getting us to comply by utilizing fear tactics, because we aren't scared any more. We are saved not soft, so we desire to do the right thing, but if you are of the world or just evil and expect to run over us, you have another thing coming. We don't care about laws if they go against the Word. You can take them and brainwash others with them, because we are saved not soft. Do not expect us to bow down with the majority any longer. We will eat the stones that you throw, and then flush them down the toilet, because we are saved not soft, don't get it twisted. Yes, we will stand on the front line for our children and say "Not this one" to anything or anyone that comes to harm them. We are no longer going to be misled by bias statistics or propaganda, just to get us to follow anyone or anything. We have allowed this world to alter our thoughts and standards for too long, and we are about to pull a "3 Hebrew Boys" on them. If you are one of the followers who are tired of being pushed over by this world and evil people, today is the day that you need to stand and refuse to take it any longer. You have the best support ever, but you have to believe. Don't be afraid of the earthly furnace behind standing for what's right, because if people knew any better, they would leave you alone, unless they

[46]

insist on sending you to the furnace and watching as you come out stronger than ever. After coming out from the furnace, this world better look out, because you will be wiser, bolder, and more faithful than ever. It may take you going through that earthly furnace to really find out who our heavenly Father is and what He can do, but in order to get there, you have to stand and let this world know that you are saved and not soft. When I stood up for what was right on a past job, my personal Judas saw the opportunity to toss me in the earthly fiery furnace. Imagine no job, a mortgage, a wife, a teenager, a premature infant, car payments, and all of that resting on my shoulders to take care of. I went in the earthly furnace and it was hot as ever. While in there, I went down to my knees often when the weight got heavy, and I even cried some nights. I sweated profusely because the heat was extreme, and I wanted to give up, but I couldn't. Every time that I went down, He would pull me up but not out. I wanted out so bad, but I needed to get more strength and time with my Father. Now I see why He walks with us in the fire, because sometimes that's the only time that He has our attention. I went through the fire and came out gold with the boldness to tell this world and every evil intentioned person that I am saved and not soft, don't get it twisted.

After spending time in that furnace, I realized that this world tries to steal our joy by making it look odd for a lover of Christ to have fun, to dance, to laugh, to listen to something other than gospel, or to have an adult beverage at a local restaurant with a spouse or others, instead of sneaking out of town to do so, because of what the people may say. I remember listening to a local radio station on a Sunday evening a few years ago. I parked to go in a convenience store and left the gospel music playing. When I came out, the station had switched over to highly profane rap and it was playing loud. I saw a few church going people looking at me and I felt the need to explain to them what had happened. I wanted them to know that I really was a Christian and I didn't play music like that. Pleasing people was a major issue that had me practicing legalism instead of the Biblical truths.

This world tries to play with our minds as well by tossing distractions in the way, causing us to forget about our children, our loved ones, and walking in our gifts. We can leave out of a funeral with the intentions on loving more, but before you know it, we are distracted by some worldly foolishness and are back to our hateful ways. We cannot let this world do us like that because we are saved not soft. It's a shame that some Christians have to walk around looking mad, just to keep someone from taking advantage of their smile. We pray hard, we fast often, and we make promises to do better when we are going through a trial, and as soon as the rain stops, so does the praying and fasting. We get so caught up in giving this world our best, that we forget our true purpose. Those same old tricks should not continue to work on us. Today, someone is coming out of that furnace and someone is getting ready to go in. Just like one of my mentors, Minister Octavious

Tookes, told me, "While in your trial, don't forget to get the lesson, or it was not worth the struggle." Meaning, there is a reason this is happening to you and you are the only one that can identify with it. If you are in the middle of some stuff now, please don't give up. You may go down to a knee and maybe both, but reach up and believe. Just don't lie down, because you may fall asleep. We already know about the Bible stories, but now it's time for people of today to share their own stories about how they got their "3 Hebrew Boys" on, went through the earthly fiery furnace, came out gold and are now able to boldly tell this world that we are saved and no longer soft.---Peace & Ubuntu, Merv

Channel 8

No Invitation Needed, Go Anyway
"The uninvited guest, seeking success"

Have you ever expected to receive an invitation from someone to attend a party or some sort of function that you were interested in, but you never received one. You may have thought about calling them to see if they forgot about you, but your pride would not let you do such a thing. The thought of just going without an invitation may have possibly caused embarrassment when you got there, so you decided not to worry about going. It made you feel real bad because you thought that they were a friend. You began to think of all the positive reasons they may not have invited you, to keep yourself from thinking negatively about their actions. Perhaps we will all experience that at least one time in our lifetime, but every day someone is not inviting us to something that can make us successful. Someone may hear about a great opportunity to make some extra cash through attending a workshop, but they refuse to inform others outside of their circle, and tell only their real close friends. If you happen to hear about a seminar of some sort, even though you were not invited, you inquire about it and they tell you that all the chairs are taken up; you need to load up your folding chair and find a corner in that room so you can listen to the same things they are listening to. I say that because I view life in high definition now and I am able to see times in my life where people did not want to invite me or inform me of opportunities that could better my future.

In 2004, I was attending North Florida Community College in Madison, Florida, where I was serving as the African American Student Union President. I would often wonder how it would be to be a motivational speaker and author that went around empowering people. I had been through a few things in my life, and I had that desire in me, but there was nothing to physically see in my community that resembled that, so I placed that dream on the back burner. One day, I was called into my instructor's office in planning for our annual black history program to help her with the choosing of a speaker for the event. We did not have to look far, because an African American male, author and speaker by the name of D. McNeal caught our attention very quickly. We priced this brother's service and then decided to fly him in to be our speaker for that year. Before he came to Madison, I was preparing myself to ask this guy all sorts of questions about becoming an author and public speaker. I prepared my lines because I knew that I had a little stuttering problem and did not want to embarrass myself. The day came and as president of the club, I was asked to meet him at the auditorium to show him around. That was indeed my honor to do so, even though I was nervous. The moment I met this guy, he made me feel comfortable. We had him speak once

[51]

that morning and once that night. I had the opportunity to watch him in action with his speaking as well as with his book signings. I was blown away at how much fun he was having while working, so I knew that this brother was my invitation to success. Before he left to head back to his city, we talked about my plans and I thanked him for being an example and asked about the possibility of him helping me to get where he was. He made me feel real good as a young entrepreneur seeking to have a better life for my family by saying yes, that he would do whatever he could to help me, and we exchanged emails. I bragged about this man to several people and could not wait to communicate with him. A few days later, I sent him a thank you email and again spoke highly of his impact, to have him respond immediately with a thank you and a few more of his inspirational lines. After I noticed that he would respond after reading his inspirational reply, I emailed him again with a question. I wanted to know if I could come down and learn from him first hand while giving my daughter and wife a different view of life. He never replied, so just like not being invited to a party, I was trying to think of all the positive reasons as to why I did not hear from him. I did not have the courage to email him again because I did not want to seem desperate or like a stalker to this dude. After a few days with no response from him, I decided to try again, but still no response. I continued to try every now and then to reach him via email, but I would never get a response, so I stopped trying. I was like "Forget it," I will just focus on what's here in my county and what I am able to physically see. One day I was in class working, when the thought hit me to just start writing. I had my laptop with me in my bag and we were having class in an auditorium, so I put my books to the side and started to type on my computer the remainder of the class. My story I was writing was so good to me, that I was still in class typing after everyone left, and then continued once I got back to my apartment. I had a pad that I would place under my bed, because my thoughts kept flowing and I was afraid of not capturing them. I would wake up in the middle of the night to place my thoughts on that pad to only transfer them to the computer that morning. I was spending a great deal of my time writing and letting nothing get in my way. Another event presented itself at the college that next year, and I was asked by my instructor to give a few words. I delivered a hand written message to a packed out building and received a standing ovation as well as a handshake from a man that I knew nothing about, Mr. David Dukes. He bragged on me and told me that I was called to do great things. It was a great feeling to have done something that I was afraid to do because of specific personal challenges. The more I wrote, the more I realized what was happening, so I decided to let college go and focus on the project that was making me feel real good about myself.

Today, I am proud to say that you're reading my third book and that as a motivational speaker; I have empowered thousands of people and also utilized my motivational traits to land professional contracts and positively affect the STD rates in our youth through teaching high impact sexual abstinence classes. I can go on and on with the accomplishments since not being invited into the book publishing world or the motivational speaking world by man, because there is much more. If you are from a small town or a big city, I want you to know that this is a very competitive world and the chance of you being invited to something great is slim unless you have connections. No one invited me to the world of contracting; I had to invite myself by doing the necessary research to get myself in the game and then promoting myself by proving to whomever, that I can do a better job than whoever else they had their eyes on. I was not invited into the book publishing industry, I had to invite myself, and three books later, I am grateful to have had the boldness to follow my dreams. No one invited me into the motivational speaking industry and no one had to give me that title. I invited myself and had the opportunity to speak to thousands of people and plan on reaching a whole lot more. See, we have depended on man so long that we will wait until that invitation comes, using that as our cue to take a step forward, and if it never comes, then we say that it's not my season. No, you don't have to be invited to success, you invite yourself. You only have one life to live, so if you take a look at your right thumb, right now, when you look back at this book, that would be about five seconds that you cannot get back, it's gone. When you decide to just go with the flow and not go when you are not invited, the chances of you

[54]

achieving the success you want is not likely. It doesn't feel good to live pay check to pay check. It doesn't feel good to not be able to buy for your children when they need or want. It doesn't feel good to have a spouse that you can't buy for when their birthday comes around. It doesn't feel good to work crazy hours and miss all of your kid's school conferences and sporting events. It doesn't feel good to have to work a job on every holiday while your family is fellowshipping with one another and the owners of the company that you work for is on vacation. It doesn't feel good to sit back and listen to someone speak about their accomplishments when it's something you had planned to do twenty years ago, but you're still waiting on your invitation from man. It doesn't feel good to dedicate years of your life and talents to a job to only be released for unconstitutional reasons. It doesn't feel good to not have the money to give to someone when they are in need. It doesn't feel good to only be able to pay your bills and do nothing else for yourself because a job is paying you what they want and not what you're worth. It's always good to be thankful for what you have in order to receive something better, so always be grateful in your pursuit of happiness, but never stop pushing for better.

If you are tired of those feelings, then you need to invite yourself to whatever upcoming meeting, college class, seminar, or workshop, that peaks your interest and waste no more of your precious time. The time you are wasting is going towards making the very people that don't want you there more comfortable, confident, and complacent in what they are doing. McDonalds never invited Burger King, Pizza Hut never invited Hungry Howie's, CNN never invited Fox News, and the White House never invited the TEA Party, but they all went anyway. How long are you going to accept the crumbs of life before realizing that there is greatness resting on the inside of you awaiting to be released to this world. Having dreadlocks and working for a residential juvenile facility endeavoring to excel was not a smart move in the minds of people. I remember one day a position came open for a program director. I was not invited to put in for it because people thought that just because I only had a high school diploma and a head full of locks that I could not get it, but I went anyway. I knew what I was capable of doing, and I knew that my actions and track record was going to speak for me and not the lack of a college degree or the negative perceptions of my dreadlocks. I received the job and proved the fact that even though you're not invited to something, it doesn't mean you're not needed there. You may not be wanted there by certain haters, but you go anyway, uninvited, and you may come out the people's champ.

Today is the day and tomorrow is too far away, so if success is what you're looking for, today you have confirmation that an earthly invitation from man is not required. So, go get yours, and if, when you show up and you're asked who you are, with boldness, tell them that you are the uninvited guest who is seeking success---Peace & Ubuntu, Merv

[56]

Channel 9

You Prayed While I Played
"A message from the once lost brothas"

I stood in front of the mirror on several occasions telling myself that I was going to do better, and I must say that I really did mean it. The next few days, I was back in front of that same mirror saying the same thing "I am going to do better." I realized that the guilty feeling that sent me to the mirror was my conscience being provoked by your late night prayers for a late night player of games that were contrary to your expectations. Your prayers were working because you closed your ears to the "he say she say" for a while from your hating friends and family who did not want to see us together…..My bad…. Your prayers were working, because you closed your ears to the truth for a while from your loving friends and family who only wanted the best for you. Even though you knew some of it was true, you did not want the reality of what they were saying and you not seeking or seeing to hinder or block your sincere prayers from penetrating through the clouds, over several planets and over "anotha," until they reached Jehovah, then made manifest on the conscience of a lost "brotha." The start of the weekend took flight, so I would pick a fight with you, to only have an insufficient excuse for what I had plotted to do. When I would return with roses and hugs, that was an indication that my playing for that weekend had reached its climax. Just like visiting a theme park, the thrill was gone after a few rides, but it was on again after I rested up and purchased another ticket or in my case until I was ticketed by temptation.

As I rolled up my sleeves to the shirt that YOU ironed, to partake in the Sunday meal that YOU prepared, before I took a seat to the spotless table that YOU cleaned, to hold the hands for grace with my children that YOU birthed, then to have YOU walk by looking like a model, all I could think was "Man, I got me a good girl, so I got to start doing better, I have all that I need in a woman right here, so I'm not going to lose her." While enjoying the luxury of positive thoughts while in your presence, they were quickly challenged by a knock at the door with a request from my homeboy. His innocent request for a ride across the tracks, allowed me another opportunity to cheat behind your back. In the streets again for one thing, but while out, decided to take a ride down Temptation Boulevard. While listening to my R&B with one thing on my mind and just a little bit of time, I formed a line to spit at you, just in case I got caught up in what I was about to do. You bought the last line or shall I say you bought the last lie, so I became a pro at confusing you with happiness just to get by. Like a dog on a mission, I ran across a chick that would overlook my doggish intentions and never mention a word about me rocking her

[58]

world. But wait a minute, doesn't she know my girl.....here we go again!!!

My untamed pituitary gland had me celebrating and flexing my ego over the premature possibility of making her neighbors know my name. Embarrassing you, taking advantage of you, neglecting your love, disrespecting your body, and placing you in unsafe situations should have made me want to confess my dirt and say goodbye to that lifestyle with a wave, but instead, I was trained to take it to my grave. I was brainwashed by this world's Alfred Kinsey approach of believing that animalistic sexual freedom was normal, so there was no need to say I'm sorry for something that's promoted and accepted in this country as a hobby. The few male role models that I thought had overcome the streets were still pimping in the dark and hiding underneath another woman's sheets. I thought that I was doing it right, when in fact; I was losing the fight in the ring of sin. While sticking & moving, and ducking & dodging was my thing, when death is the referee, nobody wins. I wanted to do better, but every time I tried, temptation would take over me, causing me to give in, give up, and give out of the little bit of fight that I had in me on your behalf. Oh yes, for some reason, my conscience had started to go to battle with temptations of mental images of you, my children and our future, but if the power and strength of my conscience was gasoline, it would have not been enough to power a motorcycle around the perimeter of a penny, so the temptation took over. "You prayed"..."I

[59]

played"…"You prayed"…"I played"…"You prayed"…"I played"… "You continued to pray"…"I continued to play"…"You prayed more"…"I played more"…"You refused to stop praying"…"I refused to stop playing"…"You prayed"… "You prayed"…"We prayed"…"We prayed more"…"I prayed"…"I prayed more"…"I FINALLY HAD THE DESIRE TO PLAY NO MORE."

You loved me more than I loved myself. Therefore, I decided to place my cleats on the raggedy shelf, next to the dumpster of lies sold to me by this world since birth. It was your prayers and love that got me in contact with a Man who sticks closer than a brother. It was your love and prayers that dusted the debris off of the Golden Rule so that it could shine in my life, allowing me to take pride in treating others how I desired to be treated. It was because of your love and prayers that I can have a family and be the best dad that I can be, and because you did me right, I will forever have your back, as well as your front, because I am now a holistic leader, and no longer an ignorant, worldly, pleasure seeking chump. I was lost, but now I'm found. Therefore, I tilt my crown to display my Royal SWAG and refuse to look back, except for a brother who lags; behind no more shall he be, as long as being my brother's keeper is tattooed in my psyche. I will never forget where I came from, so instead of me thinking I'm holier than the lost that prefer not to be found, I just let my light shine from sun up to sun down. When each day has come to an end and another one is coming, I make sure to bend my knees and pray for increased strength and safety for every praying woman. Thank you for giving us a chance to grow up mentally and love you for the Queens you are.

Thanks to all of the Queens who know how to get a prayer through, because most restored men would not be if it were not for YOU praying in the midst of the playing. The more a man realizes what he has at home, the more he is tempted. Temptation + a sexual driving world + the substance within the social norms theory + an absence of spiritual standards, only equals pain for you and fun for him. A lot of men are afraid to let go of certain friends, certain places, and certain songs, because they don't have a clue of what's going to replace it, so it takes time. Queens, never make harsh decisions based on what you see in someone else's relationship, because you may see the glory, the hugs, the kisses, opening of the door, buying of gifts, spending time together, etc., but you don't know the story of what she or he had to go through to get their relationship the way it is. Most mature men are created by women then led by God's Word just like most doggish men are created by women then led by this sinful world. What happens often is that women put in time, but because they are led by their emotions, they give up because their contentious ways of trying to get a man to change does not work. After letting him go, they eventually notice their renewed and improved ex in the arms of another woman, and that is when they wish it was possible to go

[61]

back and strengthen their relationship with our heavenly Father for discernment instead of making decisions solely out of emotions, but often, it is too late. It should never be told for any woman to take abuse from any man because that's ludicrous. We should, however, encourage them to pray and form a relationship with our heavenly Father so that they can receive divine discernment of knowing when to stay or when to go. Listening to "he say, she say" gets old. Setting up stake outs get tiresome. Fussing, cussing and extreme crying gets stressful. Playing the same games and fighting is dangerous, so if this is your way of getting him to change, are you going to be worth anything physically or mentally, once he finally decides to do so? Most men were not raised by another man to stand firm on standards, so this world becomes a training camp. The first order of business in that camp is to be self centered, then seek pleasure, so when a woman slaps, pushes, argues, and nags at a man day in and day out, he may begin to search for a short term pleasure of peace and submissiveness in another woman that often times in your eyes doesn't measure up to you, and the more you fuss and nag, the more he will perhaps utilize his wrong doing as a rightful exchange. So I will go on the record to say that there may not be a shortage of good men, but a huge shortage of praying women!!! So many women utilize their slick and disrespecting words as a weapon to cut deep into the soul of a man, and after doing it for so long, it becomes a habit that becomes hard to break. It's crazy to me that this world has gotten us so far away from the

[62]

Biblical basics, that now the basics are breathtaking. No man will ever be perfect in every area, no matter whom he is serving, but if he believe, his conscience will do its job at holding him accountable before it goes extremely far, so never stop praying. Without sincere prayer and peace, it doesn't matter your race or economic status, you will suffer and be a victim of doing what's acceptable by the masses, so let's think before going in on each other with our own perceptions as to why they do what they do. Cheating is so common now, that it has become an acceptable act within certain cultures, and people do it without any thought as to why and where it derived from. If you want a clear example of just doing something because everyone else is doing it, if I SNEEZE, why do almost every adult, even our kids say "bless you," but not when someone COUGHS? Think about it.   Most of us don't have a clue and the ones that claim to know are only assuming!! I think the SNEEZE strategy is like a fire alarm drill, a test to make sure that people are still trained to go in the same direction of the masses, but in this case away from the truth, not away from the smoke. We thank you ladies, for sticking to the Biblical basics and not giving in to worldly tactics fooling you into thinking that you could change us, or giving up on us when we could not seem to get it right.--- Peace & Ubuntu, Merv, and the once lost "brothas"

Channel 10

Get Your Own Wife Homey
"And back up off mine"

I am writing this channel for all my hard working men, who fully provide for their family the best they can, spend time with their children, love Christ, love their wife, and respect everyone, to only have a no good joker who knows your wife is married trying to hit on her. We're going to tell those cats to get their own wife and back up off ours. See as men, we already know that we can't do anything about another dude trying to come on to our queens, and to be honest, it kind of makes men feel good to know that another man wants we he has. A real man trusts his woman to make the right decision and he doesn't worry about pimp daddy. The only time a husband should get upset is when he knows the buzzard and the buzzard knows him, but even then, that's a conversation with the wife and not so much with the buzzard. If any man has an attractive wife, believe me, those buzzards are going to fly around until they can make their move. I use to hang around dudes who would be bragging on sleeping around with different women only to find out that they be shaking her husband's hand every day at work and behind his back flirting with his wife. Yes, I mean, everyday this married man made it known through his demeanor that he had marital problems, but did not know that he was shaking the hand of the source of his problems. This crap is performed in all races of people and it's crazy because Dude, if you don't want anyone bothering your wife, then leave the next man's wife alone. I have heard women tell men that they were married and the dude would say "Well, let's just be friends then," not giving any thought to the work her husband had to put in to get their family where it was. So I guess we have to know each other to be our brother's keeper!! If I am single, or married with problems, and see an attractive married woman in the mall, I need to automatically think about my brother that's married to her and place my thoughts elsewhere. A lot of our children are living in broken homes because of those buzzards that refuse to handle their own families, but try to handle another man's, causing chaos on both sides of the fence. If at any time we are around dudes who are plotting crap like this, we need to be bold enough to tell them to get their own wife and leave another's alone, because although they are only seeking sexual pleasure, those five seconds of climatic pleasure can cause a family a lifetime of pain.

Picture three dudes talking at the basketball court after shooting the hoop one late afternoon. One of the guys was telling the other two guys about this married doctor that he had been hitting on and almost got her to the point of breaking. The other two were just begging for more details. Although they did not really know each other very well other than balling at the court, he promised them that when he made the big move that he would give them all the details. The other dude just had to share his little sneaky story as well, to let them know that he got some game off the court too. He began to talk about this fine, married school teacher that he had a late night date with later on and how he was going to blow her mind. Again, the guys were hungry for the details, so he promised that if they balled the next day that he would give them the full details. During their conversation, the dude phone rang and he said to the guys, "Duty calls, this is her right here." As he answered the phone, he said her name, and immediately the dude with the first story looks lost. Once the call is over, he inquired about the woman's name and what school she taught at? After the guy told him, he was like "Hey bro, that's my sister, and dog, you can't go through with that." He began to think about his little niece and his brother-in-law and shared with the guy that his sister's family was a good family and that he did not need to mess it up. The guy asked him had he done a background check on the family of that doctor that he was trying to get to break and how good her family structure may be? There was no compromising taking place and negative emotions began to present themselves. The brother, out of anger, decided to depart from them and head to his sister's house to give her a word or two. As he was pulling up to his sister's house, he noticed his brother-in-law holding the hand of his little niece walking her in the house after picking her up from school. When he entered the house where they

[66]

were, he noticed the father helping the child with homework and trying to prepare dinner. He went to his brother in law, hugged him, shook his hand, apologized, and told him that he respected what he did for his sister and little niece. Now the brother-in-law did not know why he apologized, but he enjoyed the compliments after a long day. It took him seeing that before realizing the damage he was about to do to another man's family. After talking to his sister, he broke it off with the doctor, and encouraged her to respect whatever her husband brings to the table and to not let this world fool her anymore into thinking that the grass is greener on the other side because, he admitted that he only wanted her for sex and her husband loved her for the queen she really was.

It's amazing how we as men, don't want the things that we do to hurt someone else to ever come upon our family, but we do it anyway. If you ever see a man that's well respected by all genders in his community, I can guarantee you that he is married and that he only flirts with his wife and no other woman, especially a married one. It's time that we as men stop stealing, man up and get our own wife and back up off the next man's. If you're a man reading this and you don't feel it, then maybe you're a buzzard who feed off of dead relationships instead of praying that your brother can perhaps get some life back into it. I am aware of the affect that slavery has made on the mind of men, but if we don't encourage each other to work on doing things different, then we will continue to have families tormented by our irresponsible, selfish acts. For all my brothers who are trying to do this union the right way, I pray for your strength and celebrate your commitment to your family, even though the media doesn't celebrate healthy marriages hardly ever. If I owned a news station, my breaking news would highlight the fathers that take their children to school, the fathers that spend time with their family, the fathers who are faithful to their wives, the fathers who serve their community, the fathers who respect another man's wife, and the fathers who are taking pride in role modeling for other young men so that they can see what a real mature man looks like instead of only being told about it. The media doesn't think it's important enough to highlight healthy marriages, so they keep them in the dark, just where marriage destroying guys lurk at. The only reason that I felt confident in writing this section is because I know how we men feel about our moms, daughters and sisters, and would do anything to keep someone from taking advantage of their mind or bodies. We need to give that same respect to others, especially to our brothers who are trying their best to keep their family intact. If for some reason, a married and broken female approaches us, we need to look out for our brother by giving her a positive word and not what she really wants, because sexing her is only going to cause a bigger problem for each party. Today, we need to get our own wife fellows and back up off the next man's!!!!!---Peace & Ubuntu, Merv

Channel 11

Baby Girl, You're a Dime
"But he cheated with a nickel"

Have you ever wondered, like I have, why some men who have the most beautiful wife or girlfriend will cheat on them with another woman? Not just another woman, but one whose physical appearance can't even compare? Well, after my own struggles, I found out why and I need my young ladies to feel me on this one.

Since forever, men have been visual creatures, this means that what we see makes us feel some type of way. Once we see it, we often want it, and if we want it, we often pursue it. No words have to be passed, but that visual image alone is enough to pull us in. Ladies, I often pray for you because I know that a large portion of you try your best to look better than the next woman. I know that a large majority of you try to sex your man the right way so that his mind will stay on what you're doing to and for him. I see women messing up their skin by wearing make-up so often that they have become addicted to it and refuse to go without it. I see women barely making it from point A to point B in those high heels, suffering the pain just to look their best. A woman can have the best job making $100,000 a year and her man will cheat with a fast food employee making $12,000 a year. A woman can squeeze in those tight jeans and throw on those high heels and look like a straight diva, but her man will cheat with a PE coach who wears sweat pants and tennis shoes every day of the week including weekends. A woman can make her face up every day to where it's flawless, making her very pretty and appealing, but her man will cheat with a woman with fifth degree burns on one side of her face and a scar across her forehead. A woman can work out to get her butt plump as possible to show off and impress her man, but he will cheat with a woman whose butt is as flat as a Samsung Galaxy tablet. A woman can spend time getting her eyebrows arched, lined up, and fake eyelashes just to please that man, but he will cheat on her with a woman who is cross-eyed and has no eyebrows at all. Don't get me wrong, there isn't anything wrong with a woman looking good and taking care of herself, but I think that's only a set up when a woman is doing it to keep a man or to compete against another woman. If most men desire to be in a relationship with a dime and drool from the mouth when one passes by, what can a perceived nickel do for him?

This is a very sexual world and as long as a woman has a vagina, she can perhaps have any willing man that she wants. No woman should ever think that just because she has great looks from head to toe that her man won't cheat with someone who is not as attractive as her. Clothes these days are made to reveal body parts, so even a nickel can turn a man's eye. To be honest, the older a man gets, the more of a natural woman he searches for, so women, please be you and refuse to dress yourself up just to please a man. If you go through life thinking that the way you put it down in the bedroom or the way your hips and butt fit in those jeans is going to keep a man, wake up before your heart is broken. See, I happen to think that every woman is beautiful in her own ways, but the media has separated them out and now women place themselves on different levels. The ones who say they are dimes often look at the ones who can't measure up to their looks as being nickels or less. Sweethearts, the men see it a whole lot different, believe me. I know that if a man comes home and tells his woman that he has a new female co-worker, one of the first things that goes through her mind is "I wonder how she looks" and then she may ask, "How old is she." As long as the wife or girlfriend can see this co-worker and confirm that she does not look better than them, they don't sweat it much. If she is a dime, everything that the husband or boyfriend says about her will be examined to the max. Men don't see it like that, because that so called nickel can wear the right pants to work one day and she becomes a dime in the eyes of that man. I encourage our women to not get caught up in this system of thinking, because it only causes stress on you and causes you to not be who you are destined to be. Please don't make the mistake of placing yourself above another just because you think your hips pop a little harder, your face is much smoother, your sex is the best, your teeth are straighter, your butt is bigger, or your bank roll is longer. If any of that is used to keep a man focused on

[71]

you and you only, then you need to wake up out of that dream. You can't do anything to keep one man focused on you and only you until he has matured and respected the principle of treating others how they deserve to be treated and being with one person in a monogamous relationship. You going through all of that extra stuff just to blow his mind will cause you to do more and more, until you are practically naked, and that won't even do it, so woman up and protect your name and your legacy. If you can just be you and not measure yourself up against another, that will allow you to be comfortable with what you have and who you are. With that type of attitude coming from within, for some reason it creates a unique sexiness about a woman that even an outer appearance dime cannot measure up to. Think about this. How does it feel when you have gone above and beyond to please your boss at work and then they give that higher position to someone who did only what's required? If they would have given the position to you, then that other person would probably not have gotten upset because they saw you going extremely hard to please the boss. The point is, if a man is going to cheat on you after you have put in all of that work to make yourself look super sexy, your heart is going to be shattered worse because you may feel that you have worked so hard to keep him satisfied for him to only give his body to someone who only did less than the bare minimum. True beauty and true sexiness come from within, through your confidence and your attitude. Lean on that, and if any man wants to neglect those

[72]

attributes, then he is the fool, not you. He will be like Teddy Pendergrass, having the whole town laughing at him for being a silly fool, and losing such a good thing. See, men have figured this thing out and we know that a lot of women who feel that they have to display skin, underwear, cleavage, etc., are perhaps broken and need some verbal validation that they are looking good. That's our ticket to having a good time with them, but it's only temporary and not long term. We know that when she gets home and peels off all of that cover up, that she is no longer a physical dime, but a broken individual, and we don't care, we got what we came to get. Dressing up and looking good for the right reason is good, but to keep and please a man is a waste of time unless he has a renewed mind to not take advantage of you.

You can have a club full of half dressed women who call themselves dimes and have a woman walk in with sweat pants and a t-shirt on, only to be called a nickel by the other dimes. Now, because her beauty is within, she is confident, comfortable with whom she is, walking with a smile and a positive attitude, her sexy vibes will take over that club and the best thing about it, she will be the same person when she gets back home and prepares for bed. Open your eyes ladies, because it's deeper than what you can see.--
-Peace & Ubuntu, Merv

Channel 12

Unleash Your Hustle
"How hard will you go for YOU?"

In 2010, I was sitting at my home in Madison, Florida watching television, when a live worship service aired from a church called New Birth was about to come on. For some reason, I did not turn the channel. I was unaware of that church; but, I was a little interested in the advertised message. While watching and listening, I noticed Bishop Eddie Long bringing the Word. I had heard of him, but never knew what church he pastored. I also noticed that Dr. Martin Luther King's daughter, Bernice King, was on stage and that she was a member of that church as well. My first book, *"Word to My Kings & Queens: Achieving a Renewed & Improved Mind,"* had been out for a little over a year, and in it, I devoted a chapter to the legacy of Dr. King, so I thought about mailing a few copies to them. While searching for the Atlanta, Georgia address, I started to question myself. Why am I mailing books to them after experiencing what happened when I mailed some to other high profile individuals? I had gotten nothing back in return from them, so I decided to not send them via mail. I started thinking, "Man, people don't really care about what a person from a small town has to say, but if only I could get to them, maybe they would feel my passion for what I do and believe in. While thinking and pacing through the house, I passed by the door and noticed my car just parked in the driveway getting no attention. That's when it hit me. I called my brother who had just recently moved to Atlanta and told him to get my room ready because I was heading his way. I got things situated around the house with my family and before you knew it, I was on the interstate getting my highway hustle on. Although I was heading to Atlanta, I utilized my time to stop in the other cities to pass out my flyers and shake hands with strangers. The trip was map quested to take about four hours, but because I was taking advantage of the opportunity, of course, it took longer.

I made it to Atlanta and spent that night hanging out with my brother, explaining to him what I had planned to do. He was already familiar with the church and he agreed to drive me there first thing the next morning. Before going to bed that night, I packed up my books and personal letters to Bishop Eddie Long and Queen Bernice King. I have only attended small churches my entire life, but never before been to a mega church until that day. As we fought the traffic to get into the church, I saw all those people walking and thought "Man, if I can just speak here one time, or get them to reference my literature, I will be moving in the right direction." As we entered into the mega church, I was amazed at the atmosphere. I was even more amazed at the number of people who were in attendance. We sat through the service and all the while I was thinking of how I could get my books to them. We were so far away from them that we had to look at the flat screens to see on stage. As the service continued, a part of the service came where people lined up in the middle of the aisle, walked down to the stage, and placed an envelop there, then peeled off to the right or the left. I asked my brother what they were doing and he stated that they were possibly giving large amounts of money to the church. Everyone did not get up, the line was coming to an end, and it hit me that the time was then. I told my brother to give me an envelope. I placed a lot of love in it, sealed it up, grabbed my books, and hustled to that line. As I got closer and closer, my inner self was telling me to turn around, but I was too close to turn back. I did not know what to say and my turn was next, so I just went with it. I placed the envelope on the stage while looking up at about three body guards and the Bishop and Ms. King in the background. I stated to one of the men, "Sir, I need to get these books to Bishop and Ms. King." He replied, "No, I need you to keep it moving." I began to think on the gas it took to get there, leaving my family behind, and the importance of my literature being out there in the hands of readers. My quick response was, "No Bro, I drove too far to just turn around." He looked at me and told me to stand to the side of the stage, so I did. It was a perfect spot because as the service ended, I saw Bishop passing by heading into his chambers. We looked at each other and I said, "Bishop, I want you to check out my book, I know you will respect the

[76]

content." I held it out for him; he gave me a little smile and kept walking. That was one that I did not get, but Ms. King was on the stage talking to someone and beside me was a very generous man who had heard me trying to get Bishop's attention. He was a deacon, and when he asked me my purpose, I explained it to him. He took a copy of my book on stage and gave it to Bernice King for me. He also took the other copy and stated that he would deliver it to the chambers to Bishop as well. That day, I felt so good about myself, because I did not sit around and wait on anyone to do anything for me. I got up and got my hustle on and refused to take no for an answer. That first book became a best seller in the publishing company and it was not because anyone of them promoted it. To be honest, the two of them probably never read it, but because of my hustle, my passion, my drive and my determination, I believe the universe played into my thoughts and actions. A seed was planted that day, and it's going to one day grow. I often wonder if there was something in my book that could have enhanced the mind of those two individuals. I am pretty sure there was, but because of the way this world is set up, if you are not on a certain economic, social, or celebrity status, you can't teach some people anything. They are supposed to teach you.

When you begin to view life in HD, you will see that if you only sit around and think that someone else is going to have your best interest at heart, your dreams and goals will be buried with you. Get up and go get your hustle on. Go hard for you and don't listen to what people say you can't do. Don't let yourself talk you out of doing something that's beneficial. Put the drugs down and realize that if you are able to strategize drug deals then you are a professional and successful entrepreneur; you're just handling the wrong product. Your idea is a great idea, but most people won't tap into it, unless they are in control of it or if it's already a success. You can have a great product, but to others, you're just a wanna be, but if you hit the lottery for a million, now you are somebody to them. I want you to hustle hard when they see you as a nobody. Hustle hard when you're placed last on the list. Hustle hard while riding on an almost empty tank. Hustle hard in the morning. Hustle hard at night. Hustle hard when they tell you NO, but hustle even harder when they say YES, because that's when you show them what they have been missing out on. Unleash your hustle today!!!---Peace & Ubuntu, Merv

Channel 13

No More Free Ride$, Chip In Today!!
"It takes gas to get Dr. Kings dream to Reality"

What if Dr. King's dream was a vehicle and our actions in regards to his dream was the gas to get it to a place called reality? Reality is straight forward, with no miles associated with it. We just have to ride up on it, so we don't know how far we are from it. Do we have enough gas to get us there if add up the funds, or based on the number of people going hard, is it only enough gas to power a tractor the length of a broom handle? I feel that in order for Dr. King's dream to have the gas to ride on and eventually become a full reality, everyone has to contribute something, because times are getting rough and free rides are no longer available. In order to ride this dream until it becomes a reality, our men (black, white, Jew, Muslim, Christian, etc.) will have to chip in six dollars. The first dollar being that we will serve our heavenly Father at all times and not let the temptations of this world dictate our actions. The second dollar is that we will love our wives like God so loved the church by providing them with their needs and protecting their hearts. The third dollar is that we will love our kids and teach them the basics such as respect, love, honesty, boundaries, etc., by spending time with them instead of only sending a check through the mail. The fourth dollar is that we will keep that stability inside of the family and let nothing and no one come in between that. The fifth dollar is that we will be leaders in our community and take a stand on what's right by supporting each other instead of pulling each other down like crabs in a bucket. The sixth dollar is that we will be our brother's keeper in and out of his presence and through our actions, make him know that he is not in this spiritual fight alone.

Women of all races and religions will have to contribute four dollars, the first dollar being that you all will support your God fearing husband the very best that you can and not run him off with your verbal beat downs and your super sassiness. The second dollar is that you will put your trust in your heavenly Father and not man so that your self esteem can stay high and your discernment and intuition can remain strong. The third dollar is that you will be a supportive mother to your children, hold them accountable for their faults, and not let your over-nurturing ways for the moment become a future tragedy in their lives. The fourth dollar is that you will lead the young ladies by example in the right direction by opening your mouth and telling them what they need to hear after role modeling how to walk like a queen, talk like a queen, dress like a queen, and how to go after those goals and dreams like a queen.

Young men will have to contribute five dollars. The first dollar is that you will listen to your elders when they are trying to

[80]

teach you something for your own good, instead of thinking that you have all of the answers. The second dollar is that you will strive to be a young king by keeping a good name for yourself instead of becoming just another negative statistic. The third dollar is that you will respect every female for the queens they are no matter how you feel about them or how broken they are. The fourth dollar is that you will be responsible and accountable for the outcome of every decision you make, even if it takes you putting your life on hold. The fifth dollar is that you will seek education so that you can compete in this world of competitors and seek it for what you will learn and not earn on a job.

Young queens will have to contribute four dollars. The first dollar is that you will listen and learn from role modeling women, walk like a queen, talk like a queen, dress like a queen, and carry yourself like the queen that you were born to be. The second dollar is that you will seek an interest in something while you are young, such as reading, sports, traveling, college, etc., so you don't spend your time running behind men. A heart being broken will eventually mend, but a man having the remote to your mind will only have you waking up late in the future wondering where your life went. The third dollar is that you will respect your parents at all times and never forget what they have done for you even if it doesn't seem like much at all, and the fourth dollar is that you will strive to make it by stating daily affirmations to the mirror such as, I am beautiful, I am smart, I am intelligent, I am a dime, I am a child of the King, and I have Royal Swag, no matter what kind of obstacles you are faced with.

In order for our youth to be able to live the dream ten years from now instead of just repeating the speech, we all have to pay up or else we will not have enough gas to get us to the point of saying, "Free at last, free at last, thank God almighty we are free at last." I have my $10 dollars present every morning I wake up, because I like the front row seat and I feel just like Mrs. Rosa Parks, "I ain't giving it up." I know the men are charged with giving only $6, but I believe in giving a little extra since Dr. King, David Dukes, and many other civil rights leaders gave so much of themselves for our benefit. We have been trained to give extra money and time inside of a sanctuary because the question is always being asked "Will a man rob God?" When I see a community going to waste, but the church is going strong, my answer would have to be yes. It's easy to give money, but it's harder to convert that ten percent of money into ten percent of actions inside of the community. We are clearly robbing Him, when we let the very places where the little children play, and families stay, completely go to waste. I am glad that Jesus, David Dukes, Dr. King, and many others gave of their time and not just their money. I cannot recall not one civil rights leader or individual who went down in the history books as a change agent for having perfect attendance at church and paying tithing on time. I am grateful, but I know we can do better---Peace & Ubuntu, Merv

[82]

Channel 14

Once You're Outside The Box, You'll Refuse To Go Back In!!
"When was the last time you asked WHY?"

In my first book, I compared cows to lost young men in hopes of painting a clear picture of being locked in something and not trying to get out. When I worked at a juvenile camp, I would ride by a cow field every day on my way to work and would see the same cows walking around the same field doing the same things. I started to wonder deeply about this, because some days, they would be right by a small fence looking at the road as if they were planning the great escape. Although the fence was small, they had been trained to stay right there and not to even attempt to get out. If by any chance one of those cows would have just leaned on that fence, it probably would have come down, but the attempt was never an endeavor. Inside of the fence, perhaps they felt safe, being around family and all, and the view of cars and other things outside of that fence may have scared them. Does this sound like anyone that you may know, or is it you? The cows will eventually be killed and another calf will be born to go through the same process. How many young men do we see growing up in the hood, only knowing and seeing what's available within that hood, refusing to leave family behind, represent his block, and stay true to the game to only one day be killed?

Depending on the mentality and lifestyle of parents, a great deal of youth are born inside of a box that stays full at all times. Those youth are trained to talk a certain way, dress a certain way, and think a certain way based on how their parents lived and viewed their lives. People inside of this box don't really care to see what's on the outside of the box because they are comfortable in their thinking and daily activities. People on the outside of the box may think that the ones inside of the box are crazy because what they go through has to be painful and cause them to do things different. I stand on the record to say that spreaded pain is tolerable pain. As long as people can see others going through the same things, it's not as painful as going through it alone, so struggling becomes a norm and pain is nothing. The next time that a man shaves his head and his face, have him get his hands full of rubbing alcohol and spread it all over his head and his face at the same time. It will hurt less than if he was to just rub it on one part of his face or head.

When someone is outside of that box, they don't really base their way of living off of someone else's way. I was in that box based on my thinking years ago. When I would have the thought of doing something different, it was like someone would take the lid off the box and drop in a fifty cent raise. That would get me back to thinking inside of the box, because I was being confused with

[84]

happiness. When people are in a box, they are most often fed together so that they can feel comfortable being where they are at. When they begin to ask too many questions, or start to rock that lid, someone opens the box and drops in a stimulus check, or lowers the price of gas after keeping it raised for so long, to only bring it back to the price that we fussed about them taking it up to in the first place. The people in the box are seriously being confused with happiness, but it does not have to be that way. People in the box have been led to believe that they have to have a college degree to sit at the table with people who hold degrees. People inside of the box have been led to believe that their thoughts and their creativity are not needed. People in the box have been led to believe that getting out of the box is like a fish getting trapped out of water and that they cannot make it. I tell you that if you ever make it out of that box with your thinking, that you will not be able to go back in, because you won't fit. You won't fit because you will be looked at differently, and the fact is your spot will be taken by a new born baby that's being trained to live his or her life inside of that very same box.

Some politicians already know how this thing works, so they pull out the money and the smiles during election time, they sit inside your churches during election time, they support your events during election time, they promise to hang around win or lose during election time, but as soon as the campaign is over, you will possibly never see them again. People in the box will accept this and never question the fact that the individual was lying just to get what they wanted. When a person is thinking outside of the box, they ask a lot of questions that need answers immediately such as, how can a car salesman do a commercial on television for thirty seconds trying to sell me a car and intentionally take the last five seconds to talk so fast that I can't understand him and then expect me to purchase from him? Why do the majority of blacks work for whites instead of owning their own businesses? Why do whites own the majority of the businesses? Why do we as people say "bless you" when someone sneezes, but not when they cough? Why do we have to work eight hours everyday and forty hours a week just to make a full paycheck to provide for our families? Why do blacks consistently call each other the N word, but desire to fight when a different race of people use it? Why do we wait around until the holidays to show love to others? Why can't the republicans and democrats agree on things that are beneficial to the American people without letting the government shut down? Why do we take out loans or go broke for Christmas, then have to depend on income tax refunds to bail us out? Why was the Emancipation Proclamation signed by President Lincoln to free slaves only good for the slaves in the south and not the north? Why after the 13th Amendment of the United States Constitution was written in 1865 to abolish slavery that Mississippi refused to approve it until 1995? Why do blacks still perform watch night services the last day of the year as a tradition? Why did America take sexual advice from zoologist Alfred Kinsey? Why do the healthiest foods cost more than other food? Why does the government allow items that kill us to be sold and then turn around and allow us to be charged to get medical care? Why is the cost of living constantly going up, but jobs are not required to give yearly raises to hard working employees? Why do blacks only hear about what we can't come together to do, but never about how blacks had their own town in Tulsa, Oklahoma in the 1900's where the dollar circulated about 100 times before leaving? Why do the news stations often display breaking news if someone has died or there is a greater tragedy, but hardly ever for someone doing well in their community? Why do black history month only highlight blacks, but hardly ever the whites who bled and died for the cause? Why does every organization that's trying to get government funding have statistics that favors them? Why do we trust a man with a suit and tie on, but afraid of one whose pants are sagging? What happened to all those people who were a part of the financial scandal when President Obama took office? Why, if I steal a pair of socks, I can get arrested and charged, but if a politician steals millions, he is asked to resign and given a slap on the wrist? Why is the population of black men in this world so low, but it's the highest in prisons? Why is cancer so great in America compared to Japan? Why do regular people refuse to support regular people but complain that there isn't any support in the hood? Why was Black Wall Street really bombed in the 1900's? Why don't we hear about

[87]

the young and pregnant fifteen year old African American girl Claudette Colvin who was arrested in 1955, six months before Rosa Parks was for refusing to give up her seat on a bus? Why don't we hear about the strong women of the Women's Political Council led by Jo Ann Robinson, who was fed up and started the Bus Boycott, but only hear about Dr. King who was selected president of the Montgomery Improvement Association to lead it? Why are people who have no money overlooked and no one listens to them, but if they become rich everything they say is golden and all of a sudden people are listening? Why do people watch and listen to negativity all day and don't expect to be affected by it? Why does America spend so much money on intervention and less on prevention? Who suggested that the STD statistics be illegally tampered with in the early 1900's to scare the people for them to accept sexual education within the schools? What does the pyramid on the dollar bill stand for? Why does the Pledge of Allegiance speak about God, our money has God's name on it, but the public schools can't honor Him out loud as a requirement? Why are youth pushed hard to attend college and held accountable by society when they don't, but the colleges are not pushed hard to guarantee those same youth jobs or a career once they're done? Why does being a black person with the Tea Party guarantee you a public interview to speak? Why do men cheat on their lady but threaten to hurt the boy that cheats on his daughter? Why do some blacks still blame others for their lack of success instead of blaming themselves? And, why do politicians still receive their full pay if the government is shut down, but the other government staff that's laid off don't?

When a person begins to ask questions, they begin to grow, only because the knowledge that they receive from those answered questions will make them seek more. If you are looking around and you can see where there is no growth in your life and the fact that you are still stuck in the same place mentally, I beg you to get out of that box and begin to live. The air even smells a little different once you climb out of that box. The lid is on the box so that you can't see what's out there, letting you know that you have to lift the lid up. In other words, you can't listen to a lot of people screaming for you to just wait on God, or to stand still. You may begin to form a perception of doing nothing while someone else does it for you. No, if you don't take the necessary steps to better your life, you will never get out, and you will raise your kids to remain in that same box with you. People have often told me that they were moving to another city just to get a fresh start and to get away from the crabbing people. I love to share with them that when they get to their destination, there are crabbing people waiting for them there as well, but when the mind is renewed, the people don't matter as much anymore. This world doesn't like people thinking outside the box because it tampers with the plan, and the money flow. Look at JFK, Dr. King, Gandhi, Malcolm X, and many more. Those guys were killed because they went against the planned mission set forth by crooked people. Since then, there have been a lot of people step up and out of that box mentally and I am one of them. It gets lonely out here at times, because there is so much space and so few minds on the battlefield. If you do these five things, you will begin to make it out of that box before another doggy treat is dropped in there to confuse you with happiness.

The first thing you have to do is realize that you are in a box with your thinking and living. Secondly, you have to believe that God does not move unless you do. Thirdly, you must begin to ask questions about the simple things that seem so normal based on the number of years that you have been witnessing it. Next, is once you receive the knowledge that you have received from asking those questions, apply them to your life daily because knowledge by itself is not powerful until it's applied. Lastly, you must lead by example and bring as many people as you can out of that box, somewhat like a Harriet Tubman move. Don't accept just anything anymore because we will only be empowering those who really don't care about us or our families, but only about lining their pockets and setting their families up for greatness. Don't get this twisted, because that box is full of different races of people, and the crooks are of different races. It's no longer just about black and white, it's about wrong and right and the haves and the have nots. Get out of the box and begin to live the life of your choice because it's created by the way you think and the choices you make. --- Peace & Ubuntu, Merv

[90]

<u>Channel 15</u>

The Greatest Spiritual Attachment Is Sex
"Where is the condom for that?"

I had the pleasure of being trained to teach comprehensive sexual education classes a few years ago. I was not really sure what comprehensive meant until I attended the training. I had always talked and wrote about my experiences with sexual intercourse while attending high school and how I received an STD early on and later getting someone pregnant. I desired to encourage the youth to wait until they are ready to deal with the consequences and benefits. While attending the training, I learned that comprehensive meant teaching youth about abstinence and about proper condom use. I witnessed the condom demonstration with woody and the promotion of ways to make sex with condoms pleasurable. I quickly turned away when we were told that this course could be taught to youth ages eleven and up. I asked if there was any way that we could omit any of that and they stated, "Yes, if the school or organization did not approve of it." A friend and I got a chance to teach the first class in Madison. I had all boys and she had all girls. We decided going into the classes that we were going to omit the making sex pleasurable part, because we knew

[91]

that the parents would not approve of that, and we did not see the benefit of promoting it either. After the classes were over, the youth were asked to meet up a week or so later to answer some questions about their knowledge around sexual education. The girls sat on one side and the boys on the other, while school officials, parents and others sat out front. This was a great project, because even though we had two instructors teaching from the same curriculum, the youth responses were totally different. All of the girls' responses were geared around using protection while all of the boys' responses to the same questions were centered on abstinence. It was amazing to see those live results and it made me think deeper into this comprehensive approach. My friend taught the class just like she was trained to do, and the girls, including my daughter got the tools they needed, without a doubt. My boys on the other hand, got the same information, minus the making sex pleasurable piece, so they were equipped too. After wondering about that for a while, it was clear that the youth fed off of the instructor more so than the curriculum. I was an abstinent thinking individual teaching comprehensive classes, so although I taught them about proper condom use, my emphasis stayed on abstinence.

I know that there is a fight in government about which is ethical and unethical, so I went and got certified through my job to become a sexual risk avoidance specialist to get more knowledge. I learned so much about the history of sex and how a zoologist named Alfred Kinsey and playboy legend, Hugh Heffner, played major roles in the way sex is viewed in America. After getting the knowledge, I have to say that we are letting our youth down and have seriously given up on them. Yes, this world has always been a sexual place and it's not going to change, but when adults have the assumption that kids starting at age eleven need to know how to put on a condom and have sex with it, is straight ridiculous and should be against the law. I know that STDs are out there, I know that HIV, AIDS, and pregnancy is there, but what is teaching an eleven year old how to use a condom going to accomplish when they can't even remember to tie their shoe consistently before leaving out the house daily. Yes, I will teach comprehensive classes, because someone is in need of that information, but I am doing an injustice if I assume that every youth in the class is sexually active and my focus point is on condom use and making sex pleasurable. I write this part of my book for parents who may not be aware of what's being taught. Don't get me wrong, I do think that abstinence and comprehensive teaching is needed, but when I read where a comprehensive curriculum encourages the instructor to tell the kids to go to the store in disguise with their partner, approach the condom aisle, pick out some condoms, and when the time is right, they experiment with them. I was like "are you freaking kidding me?" How can we expect our kids to not engage in something when it's being promoted? People can't give me that crap about "If we don't give condoms to them and teach them how to use them that we are killing them." The only safe sex

[93]

is abstinence, and I think that we have forgotten what sex is for. From the beginning, sex was for a married couple to bear children, not to use as a hobby. When Eve ate from the tree of knowledge causing her husband to eat, she was cursed with the desire of longing after her husband. When someone has sexual intercourse with another, there is a spiritual attachment, whether you believe it or not, that takes place. Behind that comes mental effects and there is no condom for that the last time that I checked.

Sex was made for two people, but this world's evilness and greed have created something totally different and now our youth have to suffer for it. It is what it is, but it's also what we make it. People have become so confident and the money has become so great that they will just roll up and give ten year old kids condoms. We are creating a monster, because we are playing with the greatest spiritual attachment, trying to put our own spin on it and it is not working. Let's face it, we dropped the ball over 100 years ago and now look at us. We can't allow anyone to steal our little ones childhood days by shoving "how to place a condom on correctly to make sex safer" down their throats. The greatest protection is no sex at all until they are ready to deal with the consequences and benefits thereof, but because there is a money battle and it's considered a part of nature, our youth are caught up in the crossfire. I know that in the past abstinent approaches have been criticized for teaching youth to wait until marriage, although people are not getting married like they use to, and that if you have sex you're going to hell, but that is a thing of the past. There are some new and very passionate instructors in your town or in a town near you that's able to help with keeping the minds of your youth strong enough to desire avoiding risky situations. As a professional trainer, I have realized that it's all about the instructor and it has little to do with the curriculum. You can have a well detailed curriculum with outstanding exercises, but if the instructor is not passionate or motivated, that curriculum is nothing. Any great instructor can take any curriculum and bring some life to it. That lets me know that if we have enough passionate Sexual Risk Avoidance Specialists, we can turn this thing around even in the midst of a sexually aggressive world. I have faith and I know that it can work because we have moved our county from being 11th out of 66 counties to 40th out of 66 in Chlamydia rates in fifteen to nineteen year olds. The only curriculum we used was a comprehensive one, but we put emphasis on abstinence. The other curriculum that was being used prior to us was W.A.I.T, by an abstinence program called Live the Life, in which I delivered motivational talks on several occasions at their opening pep rallies. To see the article, please visit www.kingsqueens.org because this is not something that I heard, this is something that I helped to create. We have assumed overall that more students than not are having sex, that more youth than not are not being giving advice by adults, so it's our responsibility to just give them condoms and teach them how to wrap it up properly. A condom in the hands of

[95]

any youth is permission to have sex, just like a parent putting keys in a child's hand. Don't get upset if they take the vehicle for a test drive and cause a sexual wreck that affects their lives and the lives of other children forever. We function so much out of fear that if four girls out of one hundred get pregnant, or if just seven boys out of one hundred get an STD, we will find that cause to teach every kid how to use condoms. If we don't slow our row and stand up for our kids being kids then we are going to start seeing condoms inside lunchboxes of kindergarten students. President Obama stated in Jan, 2014, that 1 out of every 5 college girls was sexually assaulted and that something needs to be done about it. How about putting more money into prevention on the front end, through supplying communities with qualified trainers. If you can stand and say that Abstinence Education is not ethical, I question your morals, I question your ability to abstain, and I also question whether or not you have let your child go through a making sex pleasurable class with woody, or if you have any kids at all. We have taken God out of this thing and placed it in the hands of man, and it's clear that it is going so far down hill that now a better condom is in the making instead of just putting restrictions on what's sexually allowed and not allowed through the media etc., but oops, that will tamper with the billion dollar industry. It's amazing that the very same thing that we as adults struggle to control and be consistent at, we assume that kids who are still developing mentally can. No More!!!!!!--- Peace & Ubuntu, Merv

Channel 16

Their Award Winning Smile and Firm Handshake
"But carrying a hardened and deceitful heart"

When our daughter was little, my wife and I had already planned to get her braces, even before her baby teeth fell out, and we plan to do the same for our son. We know that having a great smile goes a long way in almost everything that a person does that involves communicating with others. I teach my son how to perform a mature handshake at age five because I know the importance of a firm shake when meeting another individual who values that. Although we have gotten those two things established, we would be robbing them if we did not teach them how to value the trait of being real. If they don't know how to love others in spite of differences, if they don't value another person's trust, if they don't keep their word, if they don't display the love of Christ in season and out, and if they don't lift up but only tear down others behind closed doors, then we dropped the ball somewhere and their smile and handshake will not have any hang time at all. People will begin to associate their smile with a burst of pleasure in making them think that they really care about them and the extra firm handshake with a sign of cockiness. I don't desire for my

[97]

children to live that chameleon type lifestyle, so we try our best to lead by example.

We all know of people who are pros at doing this because they practice it every day of their lives. We don't often hear people say who they don't like, but the ones who are bold enough to say it, I have much respect for them. I know that many people have spoken their minds about others on national television. Sometimes it makes me want to tell them to grow up, but now that I view life in HD, they are not the problem. In fact, we need more of them. The problem is the ones who are not bold enough to tell another group of people or a person how they really feel, but they go around displaying a smile and a firm handshake with a hardened and deceitful heart. I have witnessed some of this stuff first hand and have done it before in my own life as well. I would have an issue with someone, but I was not bold enough to go to the individual and share it with them. Instead, I would passively deal with them. You already know that you may one day run into that person whom you dislike and have not told, so it's best to go ahead and get it resolved. I have been in the grocery store on the aisle with them and could not turn around, so I gave a hand shake and smile, but my heart was hardened. One day after walking the Word a while, I had to approach an elder to tell him that I was sorry for holding a bitter grudge against him for something I heard that he said about me. I was not able to sleep and I was tired of stressing to be a chameleon when I ran across his path.

Deceit is very dangerous, so I will encourage anyone who may be struggling with a person who has rubbed you the wrong way, to please get it resolved today by telling them the truth about how you feel. If you don't like them, then tell them that, and that will keep them from questioning your intentions. The thing is that a lot of the time people don't have anything against you, they just have evil intentions, but their smile and handshakes attempt to cover up for that. These are the ones we call wolves in sheep's clothing, so please be aware of them. See, wolves in sheep clothing are supposedly serving Christ, so they have to display a gesture of love in order to continue to be considered a follower of Christ by earthly people. If they display the hate that's in their hearts in regards to you or, if they display the hate in their hearts in regards to your race of people, telling the truth about how they really feel will stop their show and mess up their strategy. I can discuss this because I once struggled with it, until I realized that there was not going to be a good end to being hateful and deceitful to others. When my conscience started to hold me accountable, I had to make changes. Now I am able to keep it real with people and I am also able to sniff out the ones who may still be suffering with it. I learned that every smile doesn't mean that you're loved and every handshake doesn't mean that you're welcomed to be there, so please pray and fast sincerely for the discernment to be able to tell the difference. If you are that person, then I encourage you to check your heart and your motives before it's too late. Our smiles

[99]

should be real, and our handshakes should be welcoming, but in order to have that, out hearts cannot be hardened or deceitful.

I remember when there was a website in Madison that used to post videos of people being arrested, articles about what was happening inside of the community, and much more. It started off real well until people were allowed to voice their opinions about the topics at hand. There was nothing wrong with people being able to voice their opinions, the problem came when they were allowed to use a fake name. We really found out how people in this town were thinking because the truth comes out when you don't have to put your name or face to the comment. That created some serious problems, because for some reason people were so ready to give the racial replies of specific articles, and the arguments went on and on. Eventually, the guy decided to take the site down for other reasons, but it could have been something great. Those chameleons took advantage of a great opportunity to cut someone down. It was sad, because we could have been sitting beside the person who tossed around some racial slurs anonymously while at a community game. It makes you not want to trust anyone, but just treat people all the same, with a long handle spoon. I will go on the record and call anyone who has to talk behind someone's back with others in a negative way or be in their face smiling but praying for their fall, a weak coward.

I have learned to judge a man by the content of his character and not by the color of his skin, because I have faced just

[100]

as many black cowards than any other race. It is easy to take someone's title and form perceptions about their level of professionalism, but don't be fooled any longer. If certain ministers can spread lies about you around town, and then smile in your face while shaking your hand and saying "My brother, my brother," you should not put it pass no one. Don't get caught up in a person's title. If they can't be real with their smiles and handshakes, then their title is no longer significant. If the DNA fingerprints results were to come back off of the knives that stabbed you in the back, you would be surprised at the number of cowards who were plotting against you. You just be real and do the right thing, because I don't care what you do or don't do, somebody is going to have something to say behind your back in a negative way, but be the first in line to smile and shake your hand. The next time someone you know doesn't like you, attempts to shake your hand and smile at you, follow through, but give them a wink of the right eye letting them know that you have already peeped them out and that they are a weak coward that's causing more confusion and harm to communities than drug dealers. Then pray for them.--- Peace & Ubuntu, Merv

Channel 17

It's Not about the Chicken and Rice
"The incognito issue"

I remember attending a meeting where the person in charge was giving out the menu for an upcoming event and it took a while for it to be approved because of the chicken and rice. Now the last time I checked, a large number of people eat chicken and rice, but come to find out there was some unresolved personal past issues that needed to be dealt with, so the chicken and rice became the replacement issue while the real issue was incognito. How often do you try to find out why someone is upset with you when you can't remember doing anything to them to inflict harm, negativity, or pain in their life? You can't seem to put a finger on it, so every little thing you hear or think that you're doing wrong you try to fix in hopes of making them happy. It's a waste of you're time because all those things you're hearing and seeing from and in people, are only distractions from the real deep rooted issue within themselves. After reading this, I want you to worry no more because it's almost all the time, not about the chicken and rice, so don't take it personal. The chicken and rice is what's perceived to be the present issue, and the current problem, but it's not.

There is no way that anyone should be mistreated, talked about, beat up, betrayed, left behind, or not supported if they only display loving acts day in and day out. So sad to say, it happens all day, every day, so we need to uncover this foolishness so that it can be identified and dealt with in a mature manner. I am going to give a few examples of people who make you say hummm, it's really not about the chicken and rice.

A female supervisor comes into work on a Monday after a long weekend and when you go to her to ask for a day off to take a family trip; she rolls her eyes and says "no, because I need you here." You have only shown prior respect to her and you do your job to the best of your ability, so she has no reason to be mad at you. You begin to try and work a little harder and stay a little later just to make her happy, but don't worry, you did nothing wrong. The supervisor's husband handed her their divorce papers before she came to work that day, and you mentioning a family trip made it worse, but that's all about her and it has nothing to do with you, making it known that it was not about the chicken and rice.

The people in your community have known that your business is running well, but they still won't come in to support your efforts. They walk past your establishment daily to purchase from another source without even considering that your products may be better. Don't worry, you have great products, they just operate out of envy, thinking that if they support you, that you will make it to the mountain top and they can't stand to see that. The fact is, it's not about you, it's all about them, so don't worry, keep doing you and know that it's not about the chicken and rice.

You are a very beautiful young lady that all the boys desire to be with, but you don't give them the time of day, even though they hover around you like bees on honey. You walk like the queen you are, you dress appropriately and you talk with sense. Because of that, it's hard for you to make friends with other girls. You constantly worry about what you can do better and what you're doing so wrong, because they say you thank that your all that and a bag of chips. I am here to tell you that it's not about the chicken and rice, they are jealous of the attention you're getting and they are afraid of your professionalism. Don't change what you are doing because it's not about you, it's all about them.

A young African American man worked his way through the ranks and became the first black president ever. He has only displayed honor, loyalty, unity, and boldness, but his counterparts would not support a great deal of things that he put out there because they didn't agree they say. The President had to go through loop holes to pass almost everything. It was not the chicken and rice that they had on the table and were directly fussing about. It was the incognito deep rooted hatred, and racism for most, and the fact that others in there, black and white, just didn't want to take orders from a black man in the leadership role. The chicken and rice (Obama Care) is what the opponents put out

[104]

there for the people to perceive as being the reason to shut down our government, but I tell you that it's far from the truth.

I had to decide to no longer beat myself up trying to find out what it is that I may be doing wrong to cause a person to feel some type of negative way about me. This world is so full of negative forces that it's like trying to piece together a puzzle with two hundred one inch pieces. If you can only take out the time to look beyond the presented or assumed issue, I promise that you will stumble upon the real issue, making it clear that it was never about the chicken and rice, especially if you are an individual who treats others how you desire to be treated. I know this may sound crazy, but if you want to know why someone really has an issue with you, start an internet blog and allow people to share their thoughts anonymously. The only problem with this is that the real issue is there, but the real person is now incognito. Crap like this makes you appreciate David Dukes, Rush Limbaugh, Bill Cosby, Al Sharpton, Kanye West, and other outspoken public figures for their boldness in this area. At least you know who it comes from. Live your life and give no thought or energy to mentally unbalanced people, whose desire it is to throw you off your "A" game. Take your next chicken and rice issue; season it with a sprinkle of love, understanding, empathy, and discernment to keep you from taking it personal. Pray for the chef, because they won't last long serving people the wrong dish. What's really cooking?--- Peace & Ubuntu, Merv

[105]

<u>Channel 18</u>

They Said This and They Said That
"But does anybody know who 'they' are?"

They don't support anything I do. They are like crabs in a bucket. They always try to hold me down. They talk about the Word, but they sure don't live it, etc., etc. That was me a while back using the word "they", and I must admit that I was on point with my complaints, but something was missing. I was focusing so much on what the people were not doing that I failed to evaluate myself to see the part that I was playing. I had to have a one on one with myself to find out that I was responsible for attracting that stuff into my life. I knew when someone was trying to work hard to get themselves into a better place in life, but I would turn my eyes and my ears as if I had no idea of what they were trying to do. When they failed, I saw an opportunity to get above them and keep them down. I have had conversations about someone who was on the rise and took another person's negative perspective of them to hopefully start a fire of lies to keep them from getting out of the box. I attended church services where I hugged and shared verbal love to many to only get out and gossip about each and every one. The more I remembered incidents like those, the more I was convinced that I was attracting that into my life. When I spoke on

[106]

"they," I was only talking about myself. I had to make changes because I was reaping what I sowed, and I desired better. While researching those behaviors, I found it to be more common in the black culture and a clear link to slavery. Over two hundred years of always being beneath others and against each other played a major role in shaping the minds of all people. It is up to us to renew our way of thinking. I remember when I wrote my first book, I was so happy to have finished something that I worked hard for, to the point that I wanted to give back. I was working at a juvenile camp that consisted of over one hundred eighty young men, and I desired to place one of my books in each cottage for free, since the establishment was not financially able to purchase them. While walking around the campus with books in my hand, an older man pulled me to the side and stated, "Merv, they were saying that you should not be writing a book because of your negative past." Without even knowing who "they" were, I immediately had the thought of retracting all of my books and doing something else, but I was too determined.

It is crazy how the same things we do to hurt people, come back to work against us. They say, "Your wife is cheating," they say, "Your husband is cheating," they say, "You need to watch your back," and they say, "You need to stop working so much," are only a few examples. So many marriages have ended because the female's friends were constantly telling the wife that they "saw her husband doing this and that in the streets." The wife never ever

[107]

knew who "they were." All she knew was that her friends really cared about her, but as soon as she divorced him, her friends would be the first in line to go by and check on him to see if he needed anything, if you get what I'm saying. It's time that we keep it real and not play around with this thing, because if you feel like me, I want to know who in the world is "THEY." The word "they" in conversations like those are clearly the thoughts or actions of the individual bringing it to you, and "they" are the one that doesn't want to see you prosper. No longer are "they" holding us back, "we" are holding us back, and "I" am the one that keeps it going. We all have choices in these times, so I encourage you to check self before using "THEY" and to check the motives of the ones bringing "THEY" news to you. How is it whenever it's something positive, they know just who said it, won it, or did it, but if it is negative you will never know who "they" are unless you have read this book to know that it's probably the person telling you and a clear reaping of what you have already sown? Peace & Ubuntu, Merv

Channel 19

I Don't Like Your Race of People
"But can you please save me out of this burning car"

Whether you're in a big city or a small town, there are those people who feel that their race is the ultimate race of people and no other race can compare. That thinking causes them to look down on others who don't look like them and place their race of people on a pedestal. There is no race of people exempt from this, but I'm writing mainly about blacks and whites. We have struggled so much over the years in America trying to find balance and worth, to the point that we are almost in competition, and still segregated in a way, but, we all supposedly worship this man named God on Sunday mornings. I know several blacks who soberly state that they don't like white people, but they love some Jesus. I also know some whites who soberly state that they don't like blacks, but they love some Jesus, too. I wonder what God they are serving that gives them permission to pick who they want to love and respect. When we are in good standings physically and financially, we can back up the fact that we only deal with and need our race of people to get things done, but keep living. The day will come when the same race of people that you hate will be the only ones there to change your life in a positive way.

[109]

I remember that midnight when our little son took ill and stopped breathing inside of our home and how we went from being sober to a mental state of panic and desperation. There was nothing that my wife and I could do to bring him back. We rushed him to the hospital, busted in the door, and the only person that I could hand our little son to was a white man. From there, he worked on our little boy as if he was his own. My little boy was a little over a month old then, and as of 2014 he is five years old and more lively than ever. If I would have wasted any time trying to find a black nurse, my son would not be here today, and I would be the blame for that tragedy. The man who saved my boy's life, Mr. HB Pemberton, lost his life to cancer a year later, but I keep a picture of him around for my family to see, and not forget who God could use to be a blessing in the time of need. No one can persuade me to hate another person because of their skin color, especially an entire race of people. I don't care what they do, what they say, or how they live. That same person or those same people that I hate will probably be the ones to save me out of that burning car.

For example, there was a rich, white man who had it all. He had the money and with a lot of money in America, comes power. His family was doing well, the kids never suffered for anything. He taught them daily to be in charge and to never run with low life people because they would only suck the life out of them. He made it clear through his actions that he only dealt with whites and that blacks needed to go back to Africa. By him having loads of money,

[110]

he was able to speak his mind in public without fear of losing anything, because all of his assets were tied up only with whites. He never thought that he would need an African American person for anything because he was blinded by money, power and hatred. The church that he attended knew of his racial issues, but because his ten percent was a significant part of their budget, they overlooked the obvious. One day while trying to take his family out of town for a family trip, he had to cross the tracks in a predominantly black neighborhood to get on the interstate. While attempting to cross that track, a train caught the right side of the vehicle causing it to roll over and catch on fire. The rich man was inside with his wife and children. He saw blacks, while positioned upside down in the burning car, running towards them. It was all in slow motion for the rich man, as he noticed a poorly dressed black man set his beer bottle down and kick in the rear window, pulling his kids to safety. He then noticed a well dressed black man with a tie on, and a teenage boy with sagging pants on, pulling his wife from the vehicle, to all of a sudden feel a tug on his shoulder from a single mother and a married woman working together to pull him out of the burning car. The rich man's money and power was not able to save his wife and children, but it took him not being in control to realize that. He has since repented and stopped playing around with God. Now he walks the Word love the way it's mentioned in the Word and not what he wanted it to be.

There was a black man in the same situation, but he had been trained by his grandparents and parents to hate all whites, because they are the reason that we have to work so hard to get what we have. They made him believe that all whites were the devil. He believed it and allowed it to be embedded within. He only shopped at black owned stores. He only bought black name brand shoes and clothing. He wanted his kids to have all black teachers, and he was always searching for the best black college to send his children to. He made it clear often that he did not like whites while attending church services. No one challenged him because of his healthy financial contributions. He had it all together in his own little world until one day his family had to be saved from a burning car by several whites who he, prior to the accident, hated. He now encourages people, by way of example, to stop the hate, don't believe the lies, and love one another.

It should not take us going through times like this to realize the importance of loving each other without looking at the color of skin. It's time that we call this crap out and stop housing it. It's only a few that are still thinking like that and if we are in their presence often while they're down grading another race, then we are just as guilty as them. Doing the right thing does not just apply during a crisis, but when life is going good as well. If you want to be saved out of your burning car situation in time, then love everyone around you and you will feel protected wherever you go. I love you, no matter what color you are---Peace & Ubuntu, Merv

Channel 20

Not This One Speech
"Parents refusing to let this world mislead their youth"

To my dear parents of this world, I am here to do one thing and one thing only, and that is to RALLY THE TROOPS!!!!! As parents, we are in a different kind of war that requires us to get off the back line and serve on the front line. No longer can we do a little and expect to receive a lot in this day and age. Being a parent has never been easy, but it has never been this hard. Each year brings about new challenges for our youth that sometimes suck them in and then spit them out down the wrong path, making it harder for them to make it back to the path they were once on. No longer can we allow this to happen to our precious children without attempting to do something about it in a proactive way. The school teachers, faculty, and staff are trying, but they can't do it by themselves. The government is trying, but they can't do it by themselves. Pastors can pray all day, but they can't do it on their actions and faith alone. Youth organizations are trying around the clock, but they can't do it by themselves either. Parents, it's going to take us, doing our part without wavering, standing up on a daily basis, and dealing with the forces that come to destroy the minds of

[113]

our kids. I am tired of hearing in the media, through meetings and conversations what parents are not doing. I am a parent therefore, I share the blame. When we begin to understand the power of the four P's in this order, Parents-Pastors-Principles-Politicians, we will understand that all of them should be working in the best interest of our kids, and for the most part I think they are. It's only when we don't lead them and do our part that our youth fall through the cracks, making them look like they are not doing their part. Well parents, enough is enough! Let's strap up mentally and do our part through prayer, fasting, faith, confidence, sacrifice, dedication, and endurance. There is no such thing as the back line anymore. There is only one line and it's the front line, and that means sometimes we are going to get hit with stuff that may knock us down, but we must get up immediately, realizing that if we stay down too long we may fall asleep. While we are snoring (making a lot of noise with no action behind it) and counting sheep, our youth are being heavily tempted by musical lyrics, rated X conversations, and visual images that this world offers them. While we count sheep, our youth are getting pregnant and making babies. While we count sheep, our youth are disrupting school functions and receiving failing grades, causing great teachers to throw in the towel and new teachers to develop bad habits in order to gain control. While we count sheep, our youth are being molested by family members, teachers, spiritual wolves, and friends of the family. While we count sheep, our youth are dodging bullets, fighting, and selling drugs in the streets. While we count sheep, our youth are being trained by professionals on how to make sex pleasurable by age eleven. While we count sheep, our youth are being bound down in jails, prisons, and juvenile programs, being stripped of their liberty, so GET UP for some, WAKE UP for others, and KEEP GOING STRONG for the rest, because the enemy wants us out of the way in order to get to our kids, but I DON'T THINK SO!!!!!! We say to the enemy, "This is MY child, and although you have a great past record of destroying the minds of our youth and tossing obstacles in parents way as distractions that cause us to struggle, lose interest in the future of our kids and fall asleep, we stand on the front line as a supportive and concerned wide awake parents with our children behind us to only tell you NOT THIS ONE!" We say to the negative forces of the streets, "NOT THIS ONE!" We say to the negative force of drugs and drug dealers, "NOT THIS ONE!" We say to the negative force of slick talking boys and perverted men who come to misuse and abuse our daughters, "NOT THIS ONE!" We say to the negative force of older women who come seeking youthful pleasures from our sons, "NOT THIS ONE!" We say to the negative force of the media that comes to replace the values that we have placed inside of our kids with lies, violence, hobby sex, greed, and hatred, "NOT THIS ONE!" We say to the negative force of sexual transmitted diseases, "NOT THIS ONE!" We say to the negative force of poverty, "Not This One!" We say to the negative force of prisons and juvenile facilities, "NOT THIS ONE!" We say to the negative force of bullying or being bullied, "NOT THIS ONE!" and we say to the negative force of racial teachings and injustice, "NOT THIS ONE!" We can expect to sometimes fall while on this journey, causing certain things to come upon our children, but that's not our fault and sometimes out of our control, because we are only human and our youth have a mind of their own. It's only when we refuse to get up and make the best out of the situation that it becomes our fault. I am calling all single mothers, all single fathers, all absent fathers, all wives, all husbands, all grandparents, all guardians, all god parents, and all step parents to stand in the gap, at least try, and say with firmness, boldness and confidence, "NOT THIS ONE!" We have to be the frontal cortex part of our kids' brains for them until theirs is fully developed, so every minute counts. We refuse to waste the 157,680 hours from birth to age eighteen by not being involved in our kids' lives, then expect them to do right. If we have several kids, we must stand for them individually, because each kid has their own individual negative forces pulling at them daily. It will not be easy, but who cares, nobody ever said that it would be. We have to go hard and say to the enemy, "NOT THIS ONE," so that one day our kids can stand on their own when we are not around and say to the enemy, "NOT THIS ONE, because I have goals and dreams, I love my life, I have purpose, I am the best, and I am loved, so it's my time to say it, and I mean it, NOT THIS ONE!" Get ready world, because the troops have been

[116]

rallied and we are taking our Kids Back, so say it with me on the count of three! NOT THIS ONE!---Peace & Ubuntu, Merv

The Most Effective Residential Juvenile Facility is The FAMILY

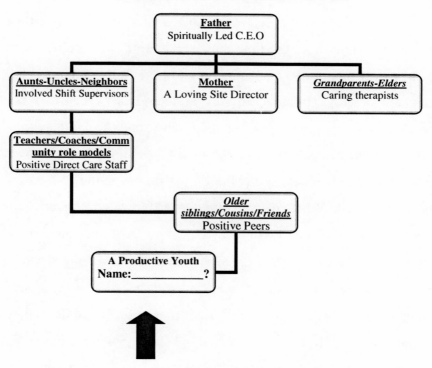

"NOT THIS ONE!!" DJJ and DOC!!!

As a former Residential Juvenile Facility Program Director, I learned first hand what it takes to produce productive youth, and it works. The solution is within the family structure. A residential juvenile facility is only people doing what family should have been doing and making money doing it. The youth are supported at these facilities; they are loved, respected, protected, held accountable, and empowered. The youth do not run the show; they are led by adults from the time they arrive, until they are released. If they ever attempt to challenge an adult, verbally or physically, they are quickly reminded to stay in their lane, because if not checked early, they will soon run the facility, and the adults will be answering to them out of fear. The family has all the tools needed, but if we wait too late to use them, that bolt is going to be very hard to loosen. When each party decides to get involved in a positive, proactive, and loving way, the chances of our youth being successful is ten times greater. I know that we have single parent households, but we have to work to get back to how it was designed to be, and stop saying that it's ok. For the adult, it may be, but for the kid, it never is! When the family/village structure is broken, it's harder for our youth to be productive, and we must expect a great deal of problems out of them. We do not need a lot of money flowing through a community to be effective; all we need is real people with loving hearts.---Peace & Ubuntu, Merv and the Boyz to Kings Family

[118]

Channel 21

Prosperity through Your Poverty
"You're a walking dollar $ign"

Now that I am able to view life in high definition, I can see how the rich continue to get richer and the poor continue to get poorer. It has nothing to do with physical poverty, but all to do with mental poverty. Whether you believe it or not, it takes people to keep another person rich. One may complain about the negative and deceitful actions of a company, to only take a shower that night with a soap product made by them. A person that doesn't read, that doesn't have any goals, that doesn't ask questions, that's quick to fall for old wives tales, etc., is mentally in poverty, and that causes physical poverty. I want to break this thing down like we are in kindergarten, so stay with me. Back in the day, mental poverty was mainly associated with one race of people, but now it has spread like wildfire to several races, making it clear that this world doesn't care how you look anymore. If you don't have the mind or resources to keep up, you will be left behind. Let's take cigarette smoking, for example. Although we know that this product is bad for our health and that it's in the top five causes of

[119]

deaths for people in the US, it's not banned or made illegal. It's allowed to remain on the market for targeted people, giving money makers a reason to continue pumping billions of dollars into a campaign to save.

In order to save someone from committing suicide with a gun, you have to take the gun away and then educate. Allowing them to keep the gun, but educating them on why they should not commit suicide is not very smart thinking, but that's fine with them, because it will generate money and a new position titled Anti Suicide Diversion Specialist. In 2009, all the states combined that were legally selling cigarettes to customers, had to tax them just like any other store item and the federal government grossed $15,753,355,199 in taxes. Convenience store owners know that if they can legally sell something that's going to hook you, then you will become a regular customer. If a doctor is paid thousands of dollars to perform surgery on a smoker, the question I ask is, would any of these sources that make money out of the deal, demand the government to stop the legal selling of tobacco products right now?

Take the wide variety of weight loss diets, pills, and exercises for example. Each month brings about a new breakthrough that can give a person that body figure they have been dreaming for, and because our favorite celebrity is involved, we purchase it. After about a month, we are looking for something else, and the makers of those items know it, therefore, they keep

[120]

something new in our face. I remember in 2011 hearing people bragging about this product that you can sprinkle over your food to help an individual lose weight. People had testimonials about it, and the company was making some serious money. In 2014, it was announced that the company was being sued for millions of dollars, for misleading the people with a fake product. You have to be kidding me! People don't do that to others, do they? It happens all the time and it will continue to happen if we don't take control of our thinking, and be more vigilant of where our dollar is going.

What about the bottled water machine, that's next to the water fountain? I have watched this thing unfold before my eyes. It's sad to see how people not asking questions, not investigating, and not thinking for themselves have done wonders for businesses, even the bottled water industry. We are paying for something that we can get free out of any local restaurant, fast food joint, school hall way, etc. I made myself a promise four years ago, that I will not buy bottled water unless I had to, but never again because it's perceived to be the safest way. I can remember being inside of the hospital lobby one day and witnessing an elderly lady walk right pass a sweating cold water fountain to only pay a dollar for bottled water. I was amazed with how that strategy has transformed the mind of the people in over a few years of consistent exposure.

Let me see if I can convince people to believe in the next big money maker to line my pockets and be able to set my family up for life. I am the CEO of a company called The Next Big Thing, and we are getting ready to have a staff meeting. Alright staff, we have gotten these people believing whatever we put out there, so we need the next big thing that will make us some money before the next person comes up with it. One of the staff members makes it clear that if the bottled water companies can come up with a strategy as bold as selling people something that they can get for free almost anywhere, we can do the same. I asked the staff what strategy could we slide pass these people? "Well, almost anything sir, but I thought that we could sell them bottled air." I asked him how could we get away with that, and he stated that, "We needed to first and foremost make up some negative stats that's going to highlight the fact that the air people breath daily is bad for their long term health." "As long as we have a few doctors, celebrities, and media companies on our side getting a portion of the cut, it may take a few years, but we will make this work." I then asked him how was we going to get the air and he stated, "Come on Sir, these people don't investigate that deep, we will create a fancy air purifier room at each of our plants that look very unique. We will have certified staff that take the bottles in the special room and seal them after five seconds. We will let people tour it often, but we will keep the special room locked leaving them with the perception that the good air is behind that locked door. We will make money, but we will not have to spend much because we will be only using the same air that they breathe daily, but who cares." I congratulated the staff and then the vision really hit me with an over flow of dollar signs. I mean an over flow of people in need of something that they perceive to not be able to live without. I envisioned professional athletes during their games being giving air breaks, where instead of them only drinking water, they would breathe our air out of a bottle and when one of them dunked; we could do a commercial on how after breathing our bottled air makes you do the impossible, and causes the breather to become The Next Big Thing. We could also be supported by the state and federal government if we can create jobs. We can place plants in different cities and employ people to package the special air, and as long as the people are working and making money, they will be our greatest promoters. The staff then stated that "After a few years of brainwashing them, we will give them the ultimate flavored air." Well team, I don't know about you, but I love me some poverty minded people because they don't question much. They believe anything from companies, and as long as they don't ask questions, we will continue to get their money, take care of our families and set our kids and grandkids up for a bright future! Before we forget, you know that we love what charity does for our image, so think of some local charities that we can give to, so that we can guarantee their support when that time comes for our bottled air to be released.

Now of course I am not the CEO of that company, but wanted to give you an example of what can be going on behind closed doors. I don't knock bottled water because I think it's beneficial for serving it's purpose, but the people have made it a necessity to buy, and as long as people request it, it's in their best interest to keep selling. Today is the day that we come out of mental poverty by thinking outside of the box, asking questions and being more aware of our surroundings. I am sharing all of this because I use to pay over $100 a month for cable that gave us about one hundred channels, but we only watched about five of those channels all together. When money started to get a little tight one month and we paid $100 for cable, just to watch five channels, we decided to let it go. We went to a high definition flat screen television and a five dollar antenna that picked up ten digital channels for free, and that took my payment from $100 to $0 a month. It sure felt good to watch playoff games on one of those ten channels for free compared to watching it for $100. I don't pick up all the good stuff, but too much of anything is not good for me. No longer do we need to allow anyone to prosper off of us by giving the perception that we have to have what everyone else has just to keep up. We can no longer be ignorant, walking dollar signs, but mature ones, that's cautious of where our money goes---Peace & Ubuntu, Merv

Channel 22

Head of the Household Blues
"Whatcha mean the refrigerator won't get cold?"

As kids, we would have specific items tear up, such as the bicycle seat cracking, the basketball going flat, the wheel of the skate board coming off, the Atari games full of dust and not playing, the big wheel front tire losing grip, etc. All of that and more happened as kids, but we were able to fix that with no problem. Those were not really big issues, but being a homeowner is a different ball game. Whether there are kids around the house or not, it's always a good idea to invest in a tool kit, warranties, and if needed, get a stress ball. If there are kids around the house, it becomes ten times more challenging. Parenting is awesome because we are the real prevention experts. We can see things before they happen, so in order to avoid paying the price of intervention, which in this case means paying for anything, we have become proactive masters. You may hear a person with head of the household blues saying things like, get off the arm of that chair boy, stop rocking back in that chair, that ain't no rocking chair, stop swinging on that door, you're going to throw it off track, stop jumping up and down in the house, you're going to knock the pictures off the wall, and the big one to make it known that we are prevention experts, before they even do it, you tell them "I wish you would." We are all about saving money, so it is imperative that we catch stuff on the front end, but I don't care how hard we try, we can't save them all. The bad thing about it is that most of the time it's the children telling you that something is not working right or not working at all, but they can't fix it. All they can do is tell Mr. or Mrs. Head of the Household. When they tell us, it's always bad timing, so we lose our proper English and immediately ask them "Whatcha mean," hoping they did not say what we thought they said even though we heard them clearly.

I remember one night, my daughter at age twelve and my niece were in our sun room hanging out while my wife and I were in another part of the house. While relaxing after having a great day, my niece came and said, "Uncle Merv, we need to see you in the sun room." Now, because of my head of household blues, I immediately asked the question, "What's wrong," because as an expert, I knew something was not right. As we entered into the sunroom, the both of them started to explain something at the same time, making it obvious that something was broken. While they tried to tell me what happened, I was looking around at the stuff that may require some major money to repair and it all seemed ok. I tuned back into their story with the premature conclusion that it couldn't be anything major. One of them trying to demonstrate how to pitch, the softball accidentally slipped off the hand and

[126]

broke the window. My first response was, "Whatcha mean?" I walked over slowly, pulled the blinders up and behold, I found glass shattered all over the place. Of course, no more softballs were allowed in the house.

When we prepare ourselves for something, it hardly ever happens. It's mostly when we are not prepared that we hear things like, "Daddy/mom, the refrigerator won't get cold," "Daddy/mom the water won't come through the faucet," "Baby, the toilet is leaking," "Honey, the AC is blowing out hot air and the dryer is not getting hot." "Whatcha mean?" Some things we know we can put off until later but others we know we have got to devote some time to getting fixed or fixing right then or the problem will become greater.

It's 9:00 p.m. on a Thursday night and the last child has taken their bath, to only inform daddy that the faucet was leaking. Daddy checked into it and noticed that it was a pretty significant leak, and if it was not fixed right then, that the water bill would be extremely high. Daddy grabbed his tool kit, and started working at replacing the stripped knob with a replacement knob that he had in storage for a leaky day. 9:45 p.m. had come around and daddy was stuck with a stripped bolt that he couldn't seem to get a grip on, and after trying several times, the water had begun to leak in larger amounts. It was 10:15 p.m. and dad had to go outside to cut the water completely off until his assumed easy fix was completed. By the time dad got back in the house it was 10:30 p.m. and all he could hear was all six children, and his wife snoring, making him even sleepier than he was before going outside. He attempted a different angle to tackle the stripped bolt and accidentally scraped his finger, causing it to bleed. Out of aggravation, he slings the screwdriver across the bathroom, cracking a piece of tile on the wall. It's 11:00 p.m. and dad just decides to go to sleep and just pay someone to fix it the next morning. As he heads to his bed, one of his children get up and tell him that they have to go to the bathroom. The first question he asks is, "Are you taking a number 1 or a number 2?" "Whatcha mean," the dad says. Back outside daddy went to cut the water back on, and decided afterwards to go ahead and stay up until the job was completely done. Dad was successful at replacing the knob finally around 1:30 a.m. and laid down for some rest around 2 a.m. to only be awakened by his wife at 7 a.m. to tell him that the cracked tile in the bathroom needs to be fixed, and that there were some left over pieces in storage. Dad was suffering with the head of the household blues so bad that whenever he would hear the shower going, he would knock on the door and tell who ever in the there "Hey, don't twist that knob too hard." That's the typical day for most head of household adults, and whether you knew it or not, it gets worse.

A single mom received a break financially by paying her car off early. Her payments were $300 a month and she knew that when she paid it off, the next month she could take that $300 and take the kids shopping. She was celebrating that last payment and feeling a little weight being lifted off of her as she received the title to her vehicle. The next week, while driving home from work, she began to hear a knock from under her hood and decided to pull over. After having the vehicle towed to a shop, she was given the news that she would need another engine. They priced one for $1,000 and $600 to install it. Her immediate response was "Whatcha mean?" Mom did not have the cash to get her car fixed, but she needed transportation being that she was the head of the household. She decided to trade in her piece of car, because the body was still in great shape, and purchased a newer more dependable car for only $305 a month for five years. The other bills around the house kept rolling in like cattle, so the chances of taking advantage of a paid off car was no longer a reality.

People can teach us so many great things, but LIFE is our greatest teacher, and although adults may suffer with the head of the household blues at times, we know that it's only making us stronger and better equipped to deal with almost anything. When I see young couples in school having babies and trying to be responsible, I greatly respect their after the act decision to take on their responsibilities, and I try to teach them about parenthood, but I can only teach them so much. I already know that LIFE is going to push me out of the way, and prepare to give them a real lesson, so I will encourage any youth reading this to remain abstinent until your mind is strong enough to deal with the head of the household responsibilities that often bring about head of the household blues.

I can almost guarantee you that while some adults are reading this awesome book, out the corner of their eyes, they can see that grandchild or that child getting ready to perform a very expensive act of mischief, and out of instinct, they say with tight lips and a deep scary voice, "I wish you would."

Now that I view life in high definition, it's easier to see life for what it really is instead of how it was painted to be. Having a family is great, but it's not for everyone. People have done some very evil things, stressing with the pressures of being responsible for someone other than themselves, especially if it was involuntary. As for my head of the household soldiers, we will just continue to go hard and count it all joy. We already know that at any given minute, we could go from enjoying a lovely day of watching television to outside wrestling with a burst water line. I seriously encourage all young people to not rush into this thing called family, until you're situated financially and mentally able to deal with losses. My sister Keyania waited until she was 32 years of age to have a family, because she wanted to finish school, start her career and be mentally prepared to be able to deal with the head of the household responsibilities. Now, she and her husband Choya are living examples, and they teach on topics such as this. Much love for the ones who have decided to hang in there even when those head of household blues were getting the best of you.---Peace & Ubuntu, Merv

Channel 23

My Personal Judas
"Thank you for helping me RISE"

When was the last time you were betrayed by someone that you were close to or that you thought cared about you? I want you to first and foremost forgive them, and then get your pencil and paper ready to write them a thank you letter. I had an encounter with my personal Judas, and my first emotion was anger, but only for a short period of time. I had to realize that just like Jesus was betrayed by Judas; it was needed in order for Him to go to the next level. I am writing this one because someone needs to know that if they don't move to the next level at the pace that they need to, someone may have to come to knock you off our track, and it may be in a seemingly nasty way.

I had worked at this juvenile camp for ten years, where I served young boys from ages nine to nineteen. My title was Program Director, with great responsibilities and in control of a lot. I had climbed the ranks from direct care staff all the way to corporate without a college degree. It was all a reflection of my passion, love, boldness, and drive. While working at that camp, I made sure to take care of the people, and they in return, had the desire and drive to take care of the youth. I was blessed with the

[131]

vision of writing a book, and I did that. Even though I was an author, I continued to put all of my time as Director into making someone else's business boom, and neglecting the calling on my life. The bills were being paid. I did not want for anything. My wife was good. My daughter was able to get what she wanted. I have to admit that I had become complacent, and spiritually deaf. My reputation grew across the camp in a positive way, and the owners often highlighted my efforts. It was a tough job that required so much of me, but my team and I were changing lives daily.

I knew that I could not go any farther up the ladder on campus, so I became more complacent at my position as Director. During a structural change to match their other programs, the owners filled the Executive Director position with a man that was about to become my Judas and change my entire life. Judas came in and made it clear what he wanted to see based on the other programs that he ran. Being the obedient person, I followed instructions. Things like that went on for a while and I was able to adjust. It hit home though, when I was challenged to harshly discipline someone for a petty offense. I refused to betray my staff, so I took the hit, and it all started to go down hill from there. Taking a stand for what's right is easily spoken, but if you can't deal with the consequences do not stand. I stood often, in a mature way, and refused to treat a person a way that I did not desire to be treated. After standing for what was right so long, the day came,

[132]

where I was called in the office and released without a proper explanation (Private Company At-Will Law). I remember leaving there in the middle of the day heading to my wife's job to let her know. That drive was painful because I was thinking about our five month old son, our daughter, my wife, my mortgage, cars, insurance, and all my other responsibilities. I shared what had happened with my wife, and she could not believe it, but it was indeed a done deal. Judas had betrayed me, but how was I going to rise to the next level? I went home and hit my knees and prayed "God, I stood for what's right, I loved your people, I respected leadership, I have been a great husband and a great father, I have never been through anything like this before. You told me in your Word that you will take care of me if I stand for what's right, and then suffer being persecuted. God, I need You now to come and see about me, because I trust You. I am great, I am successful, I have talents and gifts that you blessed me with, so now is the time to tap into them. I am in my fiery furnace just like the 3 Hebrew Boys, and I expect for you to come and be with me as well, and it's about to get hot in here, Amen." I came out of prayer with a made up mind and I refused to let anything or anyone get in the way.

I had to overcome the humility of standing in the unemployment line and being treated like a desperate individual of a few hundred dollars every two weeks. I really needed that money, so I had to do what I had to do. I had time on my hands to create the master plan and that's just what I did. I wrote a business plan with the help of a close friend and I went to work on it. I landed my first contract with the Healthy Start Coalition to utilize my leadership services. I was successful in that, the word got out and I received more contracts. I started speaking professionally, and I started writing another book. I started an organization called Boyz to Kings and partnered with the school system, the community at large, the Senior Citizen Council, and the Health Department with the help of dedicated adults. I landed a contract with the University Of South Florida to deliver services in my community and was soon hired as an employee. One day, I googled my name, and found many news articles about me in regards to events and projects that I had forgotten about. That was the day that I found understanding of the Word "Your gifts shall make room for you." I was about ready to thank my personal Judas for doing what it took to get me to follow my dreams and my goals.

Three years after my encounter with Judas, I received a phone call from him asking to have lunch. A shocking call it was, but I went anyhow. I thanked him eye to eye for what happened, and he apologized. He asked if I could help him with an upcoming project and I told him yes, but it would have to be a contract, and he agreed. Before he was able to begin that project, he was released by the company, and his life took a different route. It was because of my personal Judas that I have become a stronger believer in Christ. It is because of my personal Judas that I have risen to be a man that's walking in my true passion. It is because of my personal Judas that I have risen out of my prideful ways of not being able to ask for help when I seriously needed it. It was because of my personal Judas that I got a chance to experience the presence of my heavenly Father while in the earthly furnace with nowhere else to turn. It was because of my personal Judas that I can respect the finances that my wife brings to the table, because she was the one that held things down until I got right, and it was because of my personal Judas, that I have faith greater than the size of a mustard seed.

I remember being in a tight situation financially and like my cousin Quinton Collins says, "Things don't always line up," but I just did not have the money to pay the bills. There were delays on my contracting dollars, but Mr. Bill didn't care anything about that, he still came to see me. At one point in my life, I would have let the bottom fall out, but thanks to my personal Judas, I lost that comfortable feeling of having money to do everything that I needed and the pleasure of not needing anyone else. I needed help, so I called one of my Men of Royalty Brothers, and after telling him my situation, the money was in my account three hours later.

Everything that happens in life is not always for the bad. I could not change my circumstances, but my circumstances changed me, and now, I feel that I have that Midas touch. If it's time for you to move on and you refuse to answer that calling, there may be a Judas around the corner to help you move a little faster. I hope this helps someone, because I know it hurts. You need to know that everything is going to be ok; you just can't sit back and wait for anything or anyone. You must go out there and get it yourself with the guidance of the Word. Don't neglect the small opportunities, because they will eventually turn into bigger ones. If you have lost your job, please don't stress, because that will make the process of finding one much harder. I would encourage you to take out the time to find yourself, before trying so hard to jump back into a job. You may be lacking a personal relationship with our heavenly Father, or a good relationship with your spouse. There may be something of that nature you need to get right, that you were not able to, because that particular job consumed so much of your time and drained much of your energy. The time to get it right is available now. You may be getting ready to finally live out your dream, and your gifts are preparing themselves to make way for you as long as you believe you're ready, willing, and able to stay the course mentally and physically. Don't get angry with your personal Judas. Thank them, because they are only digging their own ditch, and the dirt that they shovel out, will be reused to bury them.---Peace & Ubuntu, Merv

Channel 24

America's Legalized Drug
"The propaganda pill"

I have only heard and seen what being addicted to cocaine and different drugs can do to the life of an individual, but I have never experienced it for myself. I thought I was going to be drug free my entire life until I started to pay closer attention to the mental affect of people battling addiction. The people who were addicted to cocaine seemed to be mentally disabled, causing them to display actions without much thought. They would continue to indulge in the very same drug that caused them to feel and act some type of way, even if they saw their world falling down around them. The drug dealers know that if they can just get them hooked on it, keeping them hooked will become the job of the addicted individual and not the dealer. I started to dig deeper into the formula of drug dealing and I came up with the fact that it's all about money, power, and mind control. I am convinced that the same formula is embedded within corporate America, families, and other governmental entities. Instead of serving the people with crack cocaine and other powerful addictive drugs, they took it to the max by serving us the propaganda pill. Propaganda means, "information, esp. of a biased or misleading nature, used to

[137]

promote or publicize a particular political cause or point of view." Remember, it's all about mind control in order to gain full control.

I want to take you back to the late 1800's and early 1900's, when sexually transmitted diseases were surfacing at growing rates within the military. Syphilis and gonorrhea were overtaking the military men. It became an embarrassment and a hazard so something needed to be done to educate everyone. The general population was not really ready for complete exposure to sexual education because they did not see a need. With the cooperation of various sources (newspaper companies, etc.), educational progressives and social hygienists, they decided to form false stats in a propagandist type strategy to scare the people into submission. Various sources in collaboration stated that 50% to 90% of all men were infected with a venereal disease. People began to give in and accept the need for sexual education, when the real issue was with horny men in the military leaving the country and bringing diseases back, causing an issue for all.

When we sit and look at television or listen to radio stations consistently, we are being indoctrinated by the source's way of viewing things, and if they are using negative propaganda, then we are being drugged with the pill. Since forever, we have only seen displayed pictures of the most powerful man to walk this earth, Jesus, painted as a white man. Whose idea was that and was there a reason for doing so? I can remember as a young man being afraid of the white policemen because I felt that they possessed the

[138]

power of God and was deserving of my respect. Even as a young man working for others, I thought that I had to respect the whites more than the blacks, because they supposedly held my ticket to success. Propaganda deals are like drug deals, repetitious acts that eventually get the addict to relinquish all self control. It's imperative that we don't go through life chasing everything funny, every violent thing, piece of gossip, blog post, or everything that has juicy drama attached to it. Please pay close attention to the next presidential campaign, or any political campaign to see how the candidates bash one another through the media with lies, and how so many people will believe it based on the number of times they hear it. We are being legally and mentally drugged by a system that's profiting off of our seemingly inability to think for ourselves. I challenge you to be bold enough to think for yourself, ask questions, and to begin viewing your life in high definition, so you can see everything clearer than how you saw it yesterday. I am afraid that if the media continues to make deaths the top stories or the breaking news, that we are all going to keep it moving, when they report of only one dying and only become sympathetic when the death toll is five or more.

Propaganda is all a part of marketing that we have to expect, but when it's used to play with the minds of people and have us to indulge in negative or evil things, that's when it becomes a problem. Please take out the time to view your next situation in high definition by asking yourself, why am I thinking

[139]

like this, why am I feeling this way about someone, or why am I doing this? I can almost guarantee that you can attach it to a propaganda campaign. People don't want to control bodies anymore, that's too much work, so they play with your mind and after playing with your mind long enough, the body will become a slave to that trained mind, making their strategy a success. This happens in families all the time, but we are quick to say, that's just how I am. It's not fair for anyone to place something on us that will limit our ability to think outside the box, but because "grandma and them" did it, we will do it too. A female said "My mama and them did not take any junk from a man, so they told me to never take it either, but to be independent." Granted, "Mama, grandma, and them" were all single and they failed to tell the young lady the truth. They wanted to have a man there, but their contentious ways ran the man off. By the girl seeing this for so long, she believed it, and now she doesn't take any junk from a man. She makes that clear up front, and today, she is single and struggles at taking care of her kids by herself. "Mama and them" did not tell her how hard it was to be independent, so it's going to take her deciding to start thinking for herself in order to shake that addiction of the propaganda pill.

Negative media and negative wives tales are legal drugs that does more harm to the mind, more so than crack cocaine. If you can't seem to think for yourself, or you continue to struggle in the same areas, you may be addicted to the propaganda pill. The only way to shake the addiction is to start thinking for yourself as soon as you can, and try not to be influenced by a negative propaganda campaign again. I will lead the NPAC (Negative Propaganda Anonymous Campaign) to save addicts, starting with myself. My name is Merv and I have been addicted to the propaganda pill for years. I plan to be clean by next year with the help of the people who love me and by me keeping my promise to start thinking for myself. Your turn!!!---Peace & Ubuntu, Merv

Channel 25

I Saved It, Then It Saved Me
"How far will you go to save your family?"

How far will a person go to protect that in which they have worked so hard to build? I don't know about you, but it disturbs me when I see a great family fall apart because of something that could have been prevented. One person in the marriage can decide to do something so outrageous that it can cause everyone to suffer. Before I got married, I was told by my counselor that every decision I made from then on needed to be thought out a lot more, because it would affect my wife and children. We sought counseling because it was required, not because we wanted to, but I was happy with the advice we were given. I was still pretty young and I will admit that I was one of those lost brothas who had a queen to pray for me while I played with her heart and mind, but I was ready to do right. I had formed a relationship with Jehovah by reading the Word for myself and fellowshipping around great people, but that was not enough to keep me out of harm's way. As I keep it real with newly married couples, older married couples, or soon to be married couples, I want you to know through this channel that you can make it as long as you equip yourself with the things you need and get rid of the things that you don't need anymore.

I have seen so many children devastated by the divorce of their parents. The lasting impact affects schools, communities, and other places where the youth may dwell. It's explainable when a couple decides to respectfully divorce because they have just grown apart or out of love with each other. Although it's not a Biblical reason to divorce, it's a mutual decision that tends to cause less stress on everyone. The problem is when a divorce is pursued out of emotions, embarrassment, hurt, or danger. The most common problem is infidelity by either the husband or the wife. I knew that men were causing great harm to their families by sleeping around with other women, but I knew that as long as I read my Bible and went to church that I would never have to worry about taking my family through any of that. I could not seem to find out just what causes these married men or ladies to bring another individual into the picture when they said vows in front of several witnesses including God. I was always told that once a married person puts that ring on, the pressure becomes ten times worse, so I investigated as to why another individual would want to get involved with a married person. I found out that a married person would not be one to tell what's going on, so the affair would be kept a secret. The married person is supposedly open for something new, because they have been with one person for a while. The married person should not have any STDs or HIV, so

[143]

using protection is not a priority. Those are not valid reasons for anyone to seek after the pleasures of a married person, but it's happening all the time and families are being destroyed.

We all have a conscience, but the thing about it is that something has to trigger it. My first two years of marriage was a challenge, because of the mindset that I had about women prior to getting married. I could not afford to do anything stupid. I would always admit that women was a weakness of mine, so I needed to watch how I carried myself, who I hung around, what I said, how I said it, how much I said, when to look a woman in the eye, how long to look her in the eye, etc, etc.

Although it would have been normal to have a chic on the side in today's time, I did not desire that for my marriage. Working at a camp where there were so many women who were not married placed much pressure on me. There was no way to pull out a Bible and read verses just to trigger my conscience, so I had some challenges, but I refused to lose my family for the same reasons that I had witnessed others lose theirs. If the devil wanted to take my family, then he was going to have to come with a different strategy, because I wanted to be able to have a marriage that lasted. It never seemed to surprise me that the very thing that attracted me to the opposite sex would appear out of no where, especially when I thought that I had it all together. Each man and woman has their own attributes in others that attract them, so no one thing will get everybody, but that thing you like about humans will present itself.

[144]

It may be the way they walk, the way they talk, the way they open the door for you, the way their eyes are shaped, the form of their lips, how quiet they are, the way their pants fit, their accent, their verbal respect for you, or how often they ask you how you're doing. The devil knows just what a person likes and he desires to catch us at a vulnerable moment to present it to us. I would read my Bible often, but when I left the house, my Bible stayed there. If I had just gotten in my car without it, I would not go back in the house to retrieve it. Now, if I was to leave my cell phone at home and get two miles down the road to finally realize that I left it, I would turn around to get it.

As I was going through my new phone trying to figure it out one day, I noticed an alert section in there where I could save several different events for every hour. I placed different reminders in there, and I began to pick up certain things on time, turn things in on time, and attend certain events on time. I realized that the alert was only to remind me of what I needed to be doing, so that's when it hit me. Although I could not take my Bible everywhere with me, I knew how to pray and I did not want to lose my family like others had, so I placed the message "Prayer Time" in every alert slot from 8am to 8pm. At the top of every hour, that alarm would go off in my pocket and I would immediately be reminded to pray. I was so happy and I felt so empowered because oftentimes once I started my day, I would not think about praying. I prayed before leaving the house and before going to bed at night,

[145]

and that was it. Those first two years were a little challenging than the rest and I did not make mature adult decisions like I should have, but I was going to do all that I could to keep my family intact. I saved the alerts, and then the alerts saved me.

Talking with a lady other than my wife a little longer than usual allowed her to tap into my weakness, and in return encouraged me to verbally act out of married character. I could see where it was going, but I was blinded with worldly pleasures, and her timing was always on point. After talking for a while, she popped the question about me visiting her. Although I had a family at home and made those vows, I was being tempted to go. While preparing myself to head her way, I heard my cell phone going off loudly. As I opened it up, I saw the flashing alert "Prayer Time." I fell to my knees and started to cry out to God, because my conscience was provoked by that alert. All I could see was the beauty of my family through mental images, so I continued to pray out loud. I realized that marriage counselors, pastors, radio hosts, and others are not with us all the time, so we have to develop personal strategies to deal with issues that arise after hours. I don't mind sharing my dumb decisions in order to help someone else avoid them. Several years later, I still have those alerts in my phone, and when it goes off, I may not fall down into a deep prayer, but I am telling Him thanks through a silent prayer, and my conscience to do the right thing is alerted. Someone could have just mistreated me, but when my alarm goes off, I immediately forgive them if I had not done so already. The more I do this, the more I realize the power of prayer.

We all have a set of friends saved in our phone that we hang out with or just communicate with often. If we are married or planning to get married, that group of friends needs to change to accountability partners. Everything that we do now needs to be in a preventive state, because we can't afford to lose something that we have worked so hard for. A few of my accountability partners from Boyz to Kings and I were visiting a city on business one weekend in 2012. It was four of us total, three married and the other engaged to be married, so we made for a pretty supportive group of guys. While preparing to leave a restaurant after eating, a waitress approached me and stated that I looked real nice to her. Before she could say anything else, my homey Bobby stepped in front of her and said "Thanks and have a nice night." Although the young lady would have been respectfully turned down by me, it was an honor to be around brothers who love me and my family enough to stand in the gap without being asked to do so. How many of us have chosen to hang around friends who don't desire to hold us accountable? They encourage you to do the wrong thing, and they come around your family daily as if they love you all. Ladies and gentlemen, we cannot afford to lose another family, so we have to go to the extreme to protect our minds and position ourselves around people who really care about us and our families. All the games, the lying, and the cheating seem so fun, but it has long term affects that often ends in tragedy. I always tell youth that being willing to change, is far better than being forced to change. So many people are forced to change their ways because they have lost their worldly swag and are no longer appealing to others. They may have undergone a major surgery, or they don't have the energy to go anymore, so they take a position at a church just to seem valued. The many lives that they have hurt, the many families, and future families that they have damaged will indeed come back on them. Making changes willingly at an early age gives you a chance to really enjoy life without any guilt. When you're up in age, the families that you have encouraged, the families that you have inspired, the marriages that you have influenced, and the number of kids that you have empowered will be what makes this world a better place.

If you are a young man or young women endeavoring to take on the married life, I want you to work together and never think that you have it all figured out, because you never will. Attach yourselves to other positive married couples, not just any married couple. Utilize your cell phone to save alerts. I don't care if it's just to remind you to kiss each other every morning. If it's worth doing, then it's worth being reminded of. When you walk in your royal swag and begin to view life in HD, you will see that worldly pleasure is only a set up for your marriage to not survive. Don't just keep people out of your business. Don't wear your "I am having problems in my marriage" emotions on your face or gossip seeking people will suck the verdict out of you. If you're having a rough time, that needs to stay within your home and only shared with the person or persons that really desire to see your family prosper. Sharing with anyone else will only make your problems bigger. When you become married adults, you should no longer have friends, but all accountability partners that expect nothing but the best for you and from you. Spend time together, pray together, laugh together, cook together, do yard work together, and much more. The more things you do together, the stronger the connection will become and the stronger your love will be for one another. Please don't let the majority of your married life be spent with home boys or home girls, but with each other. Make it known as much as you can that you're in mad love with your spouse while in the community, and let your actions back that up. I have witnessed too many men leave their wives while they were still full of energy and good looks to only get old and have no one to grow old with or to take care of them when illnesses kicked in. I have also witnessed several marriages and potential marriages go down quickly because the abuse of FACEBOOK and other social media services. If those social media services become a problem for you and your relationship, please pull the plug ASAP because it's serious and it's very addictive. Use whatever you have to use to keep you focused. If your alerts are empty, you need to fill them up with something positive. Save it and it may save you---Peace & Ubuntu, Merv

Channel 26

The Verbal Painter
"When people gossip about you and others buy it"

There was a young lady who owned a flower shop that served her community and other communities five days a week. One day, a customer entered into her establishment to purchase an item, but she was so sad to share with the customer that she was out of that particular one. The customer made the slick comment, "What's the use of having a store if you don't have what people need," and walked out. The owner did not have the chance to tell her that the school up the street was having a program and had just left her shop purchasing all one hundred of those items that she had in stock. Later on that week, a community meeting was taking place and that customer was there attending it. During the meeting, someone visiting from out of town inquired about a flower shop that they could contract with to provide services to their schools in their districts. A pleased customer of the lady in town with the flower shop mentioned her in a positive way. The unsatisfied customer went against it by telling the people that the lady in town never had anything that you need and that she refused to tell you when the next shipment was coming in. Two pictures were

[150]

verbally painted by the two individuals, but the buyers bought the painting that was painted by the unsatisfied customer, causing them to not do business with the lady in town. All they could see was a potential jacked up contract with several unhappy schools, if they contracted with her.

How often do we unknowingly paint a picture of someone to someone else before they even meet them, or about a certain situation or event? Do we ever stop and think about our motive when we are talking about the negatives instead of the positives? For some reason, painting a good picture about a person or an event costs a lot more than the painted picture of negativity because the good stays on the shelf and the negatives are what's being purchased by the buyers. I can verbally paint a thirty minute positive picture of a pastor of a church and turn around and verbally paint a one minute negative picture of him to some people. Although there was more time put into the positive picture, the buyers would rather purchase that one minute of negative painting to form their opinions about that pastor. Now that I view life in HD, I understand what it means when it's said to guide my mouth, and if I don't have anything positive to say, to not say anything at all. The media has really taken off with being able to paint a picture for the world about someone without even knowing the full story. We have seen many people accused of committing crimes, and the media will have it as the breaking news until they find out the truth. Once finding out that person is innocent, they may show it one time to the public and move on to something else. The picture has been painted in the psyche of the people, so to them, the person is still a criminal. This world has become so hungry for negativity that it takes one hundred positives to one negative to leave a positive picture in someone's mind about almost anything. With social media, it has really gotten worse, due to the amount of time it takes to spread news and the length of time that it stays on the screen.

A great restaurant can be booming with business and one day a person comes in with an old purse that they just pulled out of the closet because it matched their outfit. While having it sitting on the restaurant floor, a roach crawls out of it. When the roach makes its way fully out of that purse, it's now the property of that restaurant. When someone sees it, they complain to the owner, ask for a refund, leave immediately, and then post it on Facebook for people to not eat there ever again because it's a dirty place.

Don't get me wrong, sometimes people need to know certain negative things to protect them from specifics, but it puzzles me people just sitting around talking about the negatives in gossip form. The motives need to be questioned. Everyone has a little baggage that they are not proud of and that they wish they can undo, but that's impossible. Since word of mouth is the best form of advertisement when it comes to what we think about a product and how many people we can get to buy it, then the same has to apply to the way we verbally advertise our paintings of other people and whether or not buyers buy it. How would we like others to talk behind our backs, positively or negatively? If any of us are living a negative, stressful life and still finding the time to talk behind other people's backs in a bad way, since what goes around comes around is true, then you are really painting your own picture. The Bible mentions the power of the tongue multiple times, so it's imperative that we take heed. Wars don't start with people hitting each other, they start when people start talking war talk. A great deal of problems that surfaces in our lives is indeed linked to the choice of words that we use daily. I can even do better in this area, so while I write I am convicted. Mentally damaged people often try hard to damage the image of others. The way they see it is simple "If I don't like you, then I will paint a picture so that nobody will like you." If you allow negative gossip about another person's life to be your source of entertainment, then it is clear that your motive is to tear them down. It's normal to inform others about facts, but it is abnormal to cause others to form identical opinions as yours, if your motive is evil intended. Today we choose to use our verbal paint brush to paint a beautiful picture of someone into the psyche of others. Peace & Ubuntu, Merv

Channel 27

The Jewel From Hell
"She's fine, but buddy she's a hand full!"

There was once a man who had been married for a few years to a good Christian woman who tried her best to live the Word instead of just reading and talking about it. She would cook regularly, took care the kids, wash clothes, help the kids with their homework, etc. The husband had begun to get a little tired of his wife complaining about what he was not doing around the house, when she was only trying to make him better. He started to get tired of his wife not buying him things like she did before hand and he definitely got tired of her saying that she didn't believe in certain sexual practices. The husband started out being very appreciative of his wife, but he had some homeboys that he hung out with on a regular basis that were living life loosely and attracting different women to them. One day while hanging out with the boys at a pool party, the husband spotted a jewel heading towards him that shined as bright as the stars. She approached him and began a conversation with the husband, and they laughed like they had known each other for years. The husband had talked until his guards completely fell down, so a seed was planted and it was not going to be long before it started to grow. Once he got home, he dreaded hearing his wife complain about him not doing what he was suppose to do, so he got away from the drama and called up the jewel, and they talked the night away.

Let me break this jewel down for you, so that you can have a great understanding as to why she was considered a jewel. She was built like a coca- cola bottle, she had a flawless smile, and she appeared to be well educated. That caught the husband's eye, but what made her more of a jewel was while talking, he mentioned that he was supposed to stop by the cleaners before they closed. She stated to him that he needed to live and stop worrying about little stuff like that. She also stated that she was laid back, didn't complain about much, and loved to spoil her man with gifts. She then stated that she would do anything to please the person that she was in a relationship with. How did this woman know just what the husband wanted out of his marriage that he was not getting? The husband had begun to spend alone time with the jewel at least twice a week and everything that she promised him, she was providing. This brother was sprung out to the point that he placed the jewel over his wife and children. The husband was now bold enough to tell his wife that if she did not appreciate him, then she could get out of his life. The wife could not understand where all of that was coming from, so she continued to do what she was doing as a wife. One day the husband decided that he was going to be the one to leave. Listening to his kids cry and the wife pulling on his arm trying to keep him from leaving, he jumped in his car, and while driving, the only thing on his mind was his jewel and how much freedom he would have to spend more time around her. He called his jewel and explained to her what had happened and that he was heading her way, but she quickly told him that it was a bad night. He was stunned and did not understand, so he decided to ride by her house where there he noticed another car in her yard that did not belong to her. His body began to get cold because of the thoughts of another man with his jewel, so he decided to get a hotel and come back early in the morning to find out what was going on. When he arrived at her house unannounced that morning, he noticed the car gone, so he knocked on the door. When she opened the door, he did not recognize who she was, because each time he met up with her before she was wearing makeup. The first question he asked her was about that car, and she quickly explained to him that her sister had paid her a visit. Although he did not believe her, he overlooked that and asked her what was for breakfast. She stated that he could eat some cereal. He was there for three full days until the jewel one day decided to pull a knife on him for answering her house phone without permission. That fourth day, while laying in the bed, he started to think about his family and how much he missed the little complaining about him being irresponsible, the home cooked meals, and the respect that his wife had for her body. He had not found just a jewel, but a jewel from hell, that was there to make the grass seem a little greener on her side and he fell for it. That female turned out to be a

[156]

deranged woman who studied men and used their weaknesses and her beauty to get what she wanted, and it worked. You can make this story end however you want to, but it doesn't look good, especially for the future of those kids.

Men, this is a very important topic, because several men have lost their families because of jewels from hell, who know just what they have to do to get what they want. If you are a man with a family trying to do right, I encourage you to be careful and not let anything come in the way of you and your union. Pray for all of us men who desire to do right, because we all need it. Our wives are just right for us, so we can't be fooled anymore into thinking that the jewel from hell is flawless. The things that we don't like in our marriages came from being around each other, as compared to being with the jewel from hell twice a week for about four hours. What we leave our wives for, that jewel from hell will eventually test us in other areas, causing us to appreciate our wives' flaws and despise the jewels'. It's all about the time guys, so don't go thinking that the grass is greener on the other side if you have never walked on it. The jewel from hell can appreciate your freaky visits as long as she is able to send you back home to your wife. She will make you feel good by stroking your ego about how well you please her, but if you have to move in and walk on her grass a little while, you will see that it turns colors real fast. You will no longer be Mr. Feel Good, but a peon in the way of her finding another part time fix. If you have a wife and children who care

[157]

about you, please try your best to love them right, because we have enough falling soldiers, and way too many broken families. So many men are serving time in prison for getting caught up with those jewels from hell because the jewel decided to call rape, when all along it was consensual. The jewel from hell can come in all ages, colors, shapes, and sizes, so if you are a great athlete, a male leader, or someone with a bright future, you have to be on the look out for those jewels from hell. If they get a hold of you, they can change your entire life, and not for the good. This channel in my book is not to take up for men who deliberately throw themselves on women and little girls, because they deserve the consequences they get. If you're married, you need a man cave to go in when times get rough. If you take your problems to the bar or to the club, that jewel from hell may feel those vibes and make the move on you. Normally those types of women are the ones, who have been broken, yet healed, and prey on married men, but pray for a good husband one day. When they perhaps had a good man, they were unable to handle him, so their bad boy fantasies that became realities and their contentious ways pushed him into the arms of another woman. They are lost in this world and because they have been hurt, they don't desire the commitment anymore and their goal is to mess up any good thing that they see. That's not God, that's the devil, and yes, he knows how to pray as well, so let's be vigilant and refuse to lose our future families to the temporary pleasures of the "Jewel From Hell".---Peace & Ubuntu, Merv

[158]

Channel 28

My Brother's Keeper
"The day I stuck a dagger in slavery and perception"

If iron sharpens iron, then a great deal of us are dull, due to the fact that being my brother's keeper has only been a figure of speech and not a consistent, practiced act of service. I know that people don't like to talk much about slavery, but it has to be made known that over two hundred years of hell, torture, ownership and leadership has embedded a lot in the minds and culture of people. I commend the men who have gone against the grain to trust their fellow brothers, to support their fellow brothers, to love them, to lift them up, and to respect them for who they are and where they are at in their lives. As I view this life of mine in high definition, I can clearly see the impact that slavery has made on blacks and whites. The same tactics that were used back then to maintain the slave business is greatly affecting us today, such as the Clyde Manning strategy. A white slave owner placed a slave name Clyde Manning in charge of several more slaves to continue contributing to the mental dysfunction and trust between men. Things were not going like the owner expected it to go, so to keep himself from getting in trouble with the law, he encouraged Clyde to kill the other slaves. Black on black crime did not start in the hood, it started in slavery as one of the many strategies to keep men from trusting each other. Men were made to have sexual intercourse with several women to produce strong little boys, in hopes of keeping the money flowing for the master, so there was no such thing as stability in a black man's home. If you play table tennis long enough, it will become a hobby that you love doing. Hobby sex today has most men of all races not trusting any man around their wife or daughters.

Whites were in control of slaves, and they had the authority to create this thing called America the way they saw fit. That leadership and ownership has carried over, and if you look around it's not hard to see, but that trait has caused men to say "the white man is holding us down," so there is limited trust. Some whites refuse to follow anything that's led by blacks, and will consider getting involved only if they can call the shots, but that's a part of slavery that was embedded in their culture, and it's hard for some of them to shake it, just like it's hard for some blacks to shake the affects. I wonder if the roles were reversed, and blacks were slave masters, would we do it differently. Probably not, because greed would have perhaps affected blacks as well, and caused us to misuse and abuse the human product for more financial gain. We would have the black KKK, the Black House, where whites would be celebrating their first white president in

[160]

2008. Most businesses would be owned by blacks and the tea party would be majority blacks trying to keep things from changing.

I can go on an on about reasons why men are the way we are and they would be valid, but it's time for us to let go and begin to live this thing out called "My brother's keeper," instead of only talking about it. I am my brother's keeper, because I will support everything positive that you are doing, no matter your race. I am my brother's keeper, because I will respect your wife in and out of your presence. I am my brother's keeper, because I will be there financially to catch you if you are ever in need, and I am able. I am my brother's keeper, because I will hold you accountable at all times to the best of my ability while on my watch, so that you don't do anything stupid to lose what you have worked so hard for. I am my brother's keeper, because I refuse to have anyone talk negative about you behind your back. I am my brother's keeper because you can trust me around all of your kids, and know that if anything ever happens to you that I will do all that I can to keep your family going forward. I am my brother's keeper because I will not do anything around you that will tempt you or offend you. I am my brother's keeper because I am not afraid to hug you and say that I love you.

We started a men of royalty network to give men a spot where we can support one another, and where young men can get guidance from several men if they don't have a father to turn to. This network is really awesome, because men have to sign up for it, and if any man has a product to sell or something going on, they can advertise it on there and I encourage every man on there to get involved and support each other. We as men don't really believe in supporting things like we should, so I wanted to create a place where every man would know that he will automatically get the support and love needed to get him through. There's nothing like coming out with a cd, a book, other products, having a marital problem, a financial problem, etc., and knowing that you already have a gang of men, who, if nobody supports you, they will. I am thankful for Men of Royalty, and I will continue to add more men and young boys to it. Brothers, we can't continue to walk this life as if we can do it by ourselves. We need each other more than we think. Viewing life in HD has allowed me to cut through perception and see the reality of male judges, principles, teachers, NFL players, NBA players, professional coaches, bishops, pastors, MLB players, popes, senators, presidents, actors, musicians, comedians, cops, etc., to see that all men suffer, struggle, fall and need other men to be there that will stand and really mean it. That is what it means to be a brother's keeper.

When I was a kid, the perception of those men in highlighted areas was that they had it all together, and today, some highlighted men fall because they perceive it to be that way themselves. Picture me, Merv T., a blue collar author living in a small town, giving marriage advice to Bishop Eddie Long, and him receiving it. That doesn't sound right, because we have made it that way. I learned to see it differently when I got advice from a man that sold hotdogs on the corner for a living. I don't care about race, social status, political power, amount of money or fame, we all need each other. There is a dagger that we must all stick inside of slavery and perception, if we want to be able to trust each other, work together, support each other, and truly be "My brother's keeper."

I get tired of seeing men come out of prison with temporary muscles and maturity, to only lose it once the reality of freedom sinks in. It doesn't take any of us going to prison just to get ripped through working out. Organize community work outs with your positive brothers. It doesn't take going to prison to learn about the Bible and find God. Get involved with a few brothers who love the Lord inside of the community instead of behind bars. It doesn't take any of us robbing another just to make ends meet. Build trust with other brothers and watch how they lend it to you instead of you taking it from another. It doesn't take any of us losing our families through infidelity. Hang around men who desire to hold us accountable to make the right decisions instead of hanging around ones who will assist us in doing the wrong things. You must know brother, that there are men out here that will be there for you and that you are not in this fight alone. The day that men quit only talking about being my brother's keeper and start to live it, we will see a shift in the atmosphere, causing more communities to prosper. I am "My brother's keeper"---Peace & Ubuntu, Merv

Channel 29

All It Takes is One, Is It YOU?
"The day you decide to get your Dukes on"

It is my honor to dedicate this channel to a leader, a champion, a small town hero, a father, a mentor and Madison County, Florida's civil rights activist, Mr. David Dukes. I did a lot of research on this brother and even had some personal encounters with him. During the civil rights movement, Mr. Dukes was chosen to stand at a time when standing often meant death. He led sit-ins, marches, and community meetings to bring more awareness to the fact that everyone needed to be treated equal and respected on a daily basis for the character that they displayed. Through reading his books and talking with him in person, there were several times on his chosen journey that he had to stand alone. This brother did not show any fear, he did not lower his standards just to get support, he refused to walk in defeat even when the odds were against him, and he never backed down from a challenge that stood in the way of his ordained mission, no matter how educated or financially powerful the opponent was. You would think by him standing and going so hard for the people, that would make him the peoples champ, but for some reason, it caused people to be against him. I found out that when you are chosen to carry out a mission, there are people also who have been there for a while, carrying out a mission to keep things the same way. There are people who are carrying out the mission to raise their kids to live in the same mental rut that they are in. There are people also carrying out the mission of profiting off of another's ignorance, so your mission becomes a burden to some, because they don't see any other way than the way they have been seeing it. Change doesn't fall out of the sky; it comes through the work of people. When we hear the saying that people hate change, if you are the change agent, get ready to be hated. Mr. Dukes was a change agent, and today, several of the young men that he touched are now not serving time in prison, but married with children, homes, businesses, and are leaders in their communities. All it took was one to stand, and he was chosen to carry out that mission. Now, his actions have struck a match under several, giving us power to know that there is power in one. The Boyz to Kings Family conducted a David Dukes "Get Your Dukes On" flag football tournament in 2013, where we had youth do poster projects about this powerful man. During each game, we read facts about him, so the children will know about this brother's contributions, despite the feelings of others who may have been feeling some type of way, because his mission caused them to step up or step out of the way of blocking success in a small town that was in great need of change. All it took was one to stand, so what are you waiting for? While typing this part of my book, the news station aired live

[165]

footage of the people in Africa mourning over the death of Mr. Nelson Mandela. They were giving praises on how much love and passion one man possessed. One person being interviewed stated that all it took was one and Mandela was the one, and then they started to talk about my brother Gandhi. I would have loved to look those guys in the eye, just to take a peak at their souls, because they were not your everyday people, just like Mr. Dukes.

It's something about small towns and giving recognition when it is due, but it's common to create statues, create street names, create a special day, or to name a building after someone who deserves credit, after they are dead and no longer around to touch. As of 2014, Mr. Dukes is alive and well, living in Miami Florida with his family, still being a blessing to youth and families. We are going to rep our chosen one while the breath is still in his body. We have become accustomed to representing and highlighting professional athletes over people who have paved the way, and it's clearly a perception of money over maintenance.

If you are the chosen one, please stand and get your Dukes on, by going hard each and every day, letting your little light shine and refusing to ever let it go dim. If you are the chosen one, you know it, you feel it, you have confirmed it, you see it, but you don't believe it. If you are walking or riding around your community, and it bothers you to see things going the way that they are going, and you have ideas to fix the problem, you may be the one chosen to carry out that task. Don't sit back any longer and allow your community to suffer because it's convenient for others. Get up and get your Dukes on by being that change agent. All it takes is one, and eventually, people will follow your vision, as long as you stay on the front line leading by example. You owe this to your kids and other kids that don't deserve to grow up in an environment that's not going to be supportive or beneficial to their dreams and goals. If Gandhi's quote "I am who I am because of who we are" is true, then why would we want our kids to grow up in a community that's not moving forward.

Don't be distracted by the assumption that it takes money to bring about change, because it does not. All it takes is love, passion, determination, faith, humbleness, the ability to follow, as well as the ability to lead. I got tired of seeing grant money come through a community and cause a fire to be started under people, to soon be put out when the money is gone, so my God directed me to step out on faith. I started a Boyz to Kings Organization without any grant money or consistent money from any one source. I was led to get sustainability on the front end with dedicated people instead of waiting or expecting to get it on the back end with money, and it worked. One person stepped out there on faith and now we have several adults on board helping to make that vision possible of having a village again. Boyz to Kings has partnered with community businesses; we have spoken in front of policy makers, built ramps for elders, generated annual events for the community to take part in, and so much more. As of 2014, we have yet to receive a grant and we started in 2010. The strategy from the beginning was to use the power of the people, because we are all walking curriculums. We just have to be willing let people flip through our pages to learn from us. The people can take care of each other, so when it's time for events, the parents have to be involved and support their own youth with the support of others. That way, it doesn't give them a chance to take a back seat. I can go on and on about Boyz to Kings, but the point is, it took me deciding to stand and say, "No more!" If I was not helping better the problem in my community by getting involved, my inactive status would have been contributing to the problem. We are training young men to respect their elders, to respect every Queen, to never give up, to accept accountability, to display proper appearance, to stay physically fit, to take pride in reading literature, etc.

How many more young people are you going to watch come through that community pipeline to mental poverty and do nothing about it? You know who you are and the time is now for you to stand and get your Dukes on. Everybody is not going to step up, so despite your age, if you are the one, please take on the challenge. If you are someone reading this book and know of someone who is trying to make a difference with the right motives, I challenge you to get behind their efforts by motivating them, supporting their events, sending more positive people their way and not talking behind their backs in a negative way.

When you do decide to get your Dukes on, I will warn you that some of the same people, who have been preaching about change but not putting forth any actions, will be the first to stab you in the back. Keep pushing and don't let anything stop you. The more I see the progress of Boyz to Kings, the more I am convinced that we may not be ordained to be around forever, but used temporarily as an example for others to see that it do not take waiting on a grant, a professional athletes money, or wealthy individuals to bring about change in a community. All it takes is one person with love, passion, determination, vision, boldness, faith, etc, deciding to get their Dukes on, and refusing to give up, even when the people are not ready to get behind it. Thank you Mr. Dukes for teaching an entire county of people what true bravery and being a servant means. People sing the song "Give myself away, so You can use me" and it sounds so good, but it will sound a whole lot better if it was to be lived out instead of only being sung. All it takes is one, so what are you waiting on, start getting your Dukes on today.---Peace & Ubuntu, Merv

Channel 30

Who Am I
"The benefits of a girl having her father in her life"
By: My daughter, Lyric Mattair

Who are you? Are you that little girl suffering from low self esteem; are you that little girl who's dealing with depression, failure, holes, scrapes, bruises, and guilt? Who are you? Are you that little girl that's afraid to take off the mask? Are you that girl that's afraid to branch off and show who she really is? Who's scared to be talked about, who's scared to fail at something, who thinks she can't enjoy life? Who are you? Are you that girl who's trying to cover up all the open wounds, all the down talks, the mistreats? Who are you? What is it that you're running from or what is it that you're afraid of? Oftentimes we try to imitate someone we're really not, when in reality we're lost, trying to find our inner self. If the make-up, eye shadow, eyelashes, eyeliner, mascara, nails, and the weave makes you feel beautiful, then how do you feel without it? Is it a feeling of insecurity, dejection, or maybe fear? What is it that you're really trying to fix that's so wrong? No need to fix what God has already worked on. Sometimes the person you see everyday in the mirror may not be what others see. Being yourself does not only deal with you're

[170]

outer beauty, but being you is what simply defines who you are. Sometimes it just takes staring in the mirror, asking yourself who am I? Am I what God wants me to be or am I what the world wants to see. True beauty is not in the figure you carry nor is it in the clothes you wear. It's about being comfortable in your own skin. It's not the fancy hair, gold jewelry, or fine clothes that should define your beauty. The beauty is not related to what color you are or what color your eyes are. True beauty is about who you are as a human being, your principles, and moral compass. So again, the question is, who are you? Well that's easy. You're a beautiful, independent, and unbreakable girl. You are a girl with hope, one who never gives up, a girl who never stops trying. More like an independent and incredible girl. A girl that knows her worth and who she really is, but not who she pretends to be. A girl that will always be happy with what she has, one with many possibilities. A girl that will never be someone she's not. So again, don't be afraid to show who you really are, because no one is picture perfect, but we're all worth the picture still.

The main purpose of this section is to develop and understand the benefits of having a father figure active and effectively involved. Whether you are a girl with no father, a single mother, or a father that doesn't think it's important to be a part of a young girl's life, and reading this section, this is rightfully for you. Having a father active in you're life is one of the greatest feelings ever. Why? Because a father can teach many things that a mother just cannot. From love, importance of having respect for your temple, outreach towards young men, and the biggest of them all, protection. Every girl wants to feel protected, they want to be able to say they have that guy that's going to look after them, get them out of trouble, and be their biggest support system. Unfortunately, every girl doesn't know that feeling, so they try to find it elsewhere. Many girls suffer from low self esteem, disappointment, and emptiness because of the absence of their father. They tend to find everything they can, to cover up all the pain so they can feel loved. But the love they tend to be receiving is nothing compared to a father's love. Therefore the love she gets elsewhere just may be the only love she knows, why? Because she didn't have a father to tell her how boys think, what to do if a boy breaks her heart, show her how a young man is supposed to treat her, take her out on little dates, buy her things, spoil her, give her money, protect her, and show her how love really feels. It baffles me to know that so many girls are fatherless, because that's one of the biggest factors to a girl's life, and knowing that a majority of them are missing it, really confounds me. I think that it's time for fathers to swallow their pride, own up to their responsibilities and be a man. We are losing too many of our girls, because fathers decided to take the easy way out or because mothers don't appreciate what the father is bringing to the table and pushes him away. It hurts me to see young girls' lives go down the drain when most of it could've been prevented. Just maybe some rules,

[172]

expectations, and consistency can and could have saved many girls' lives. I don't know how it feels to be fatherless, but I do know how it feels to have not only a father, but a committed one. Just knowing I have someone that has my back, I can trust, spend time with, learn from, and rely on is one of the greatest feelings to have. Knowing that I am an 18 year old senior in high school that won Miss Junior, Miss MCHS, Homecoming princess, graduating with my diploma, not pregnant, still a virgin, and one who will stand behind the abstinence message in spite of living in a world that encourages me to Just Wrap It Up, goes to show that having an active and committed father a part of a young girl's life does pays off. Not only did having my dad there bless me, but having him and my mom work through tough times together instead of giving up on each other allows me to place the value of family on a higher pedestal and not be so easy to give up. I can't make the statement that I don't need a man, because my dad displayed the true benefits of having a Godly man around, so I want one just like him or better. Thanks for reading and I hope that some young girl can grow up and experience the true benefits of having a father in her life each and every day. Thanks Pops!!!

Channel 31

Christ Paid the Cashier of Life
"And we say "KEEP THE CHANGE"

I can remember back in my younger days, my boy Williams and I would take turns leaving the job to purchase dinner from different food establishments. We had both created a habit of after paying for the food, telling the cashier to keep the change. We did this for a long time, because we did not have many responsibilities. We did not see how letting something that belonged to us remain in another's possession could cause any problems in our lives. One would come back and the other would ask where the $5 of change was, and the answer would always be, I told them to keep the change. Our children started getting older, the bills kept rolling in, gas started getting higher, and so much more, and so we started being conscious of what belonged to us and how every bit counted. The older we got, the more mature we got, and the more responsibilities that we got, so we automatically accepted our change and if it was not the right amount, we would go back until we got what belonged to us.

I shared that little history because it reminds me of the greatest man to ever walk this earth, and the amount of power that each of us holds because of His efforts. I have been on this earth

[174]

thirty-five years and always said that there had to be something different to the good ole way of living. We have all been a product of our environment at some point of our lives and some are still wearing that bar code. If our family worked the mills forever, for some reason, our mind tells us that we have to work there as well. If our parents did not believe in stability inside of a family, we may not place value on it. If our daddy only pimped the women and never committed to one, we may do our share of pimping. If mom utilized her body through prostitution to keep from standing in the welfare line, you may walk in her shoes when times get tough. If you lived in a violent neighborhood where hatred was the norm, you may take pride in cracking someone's forehead. If you have witnessed nothing but financial struggles in your family, you may have an unbalanced view of success. If you have witnessed the only men you know serve time in and out of prison and then giving parties when they got out, you may think going to prison is a part of being considered a real man. If you have been raised in a family church where all you hear is a lot of complaining, and see a lot of mental and physical poverty, you may grow up thinking that Christians are supposed to suffer and not have much. If you have witnessed women run their household and taking care of their kids alone, you also may grow up thinking that you can be an independent woman that doesn't need a man to help take care of you or your kids. If your bar code was scanned today, what section would you belong to?

It is common to not accept change in certain environments because we become so use to doing what we think is pleasing to someone else, but when it starts to hurt and affect our goals and dreams, who can we turn to? This is my book, so I desire to tell you the truth and not just what sells. After reading my Bible, comprehending my Bible, applying my knowledge, fasting and praying, I can now see life in HD. The Bible is the road map to our mental growth, not college or money. When Christ died for us, He paid for everything but we have to get the change ourselves. If the universe is ours, then in our thinking we can get our change. I want my change because I am tired of barely making it and I deserve better. If my change is in my thinking and this universe have been paid for, then I need the exact change and I need it now. I got tired running the streets and mistreating the ones that I love, so I went and got my change. I got tired of talking behind another person's back and then shaking their hands and smiling in their face, so I went and got my change. I got tired of believing that if I don't tithe, I am going to hell, but if I mistreat my brothers and sisters in Christ it will be forgiven, so I went and got my change. I got tired of viewing my Queens as sex toys, so I went and got my change. I got tired of living the life of a small town pimp and having the potential of causing my daughter to grow up looking for a man like me, so I went and got my change. I got tired of people making me believe that I should hate all white people because a select few display hate towards all of us, so I went and got my change. I got

[176]

tired of stabbing my brothers and sisters in the back, so I went and got my change. I got tired of being tricked into thinking that I should not pursue my dreams because there is not enough wealth to go around, so I went and got my change. I got tired of blaming others for my shortcomings and not looking at myself, so I went and got my change. I got tired of working a job trying to please a man instead of God, so I went and got my change. I got tired of people making me believe that everything I did should be catered to blacks only, so I went and got my change. I got tired of being told because I am black, that I must vote democrat, without examining the character of the candidate running, so I went and got my change. I got tired of consistently listening to negativity through the media and having my thoughts and actions suffer from it, so I went and got my change. We only have one life to live and the hand of time is not going counter clockwise. How long are we going to let our change sit out there before we realize that it's ours and we need it NOW? It's ok to be generous with our giving, but if this universe is holding the change that we need to get us to the next level, it is pay day baby, and the success bill is past due.

We can't be fooled any longer to think that we can just sit back and wait on God, or just be still and expect our dreams become a full reality. It is also vital that we be aware of people misusing the word patience so often in their daily conversations. Lazy people use patience the most as a crutch to stay where they are in life, but if you evaluate their life, you may see where their over indulgence into patience has converted into insanity. They do the same things everyday but expect something different to happen. Get up and get that change today if you're tired of coming up short. Sitting back waiting on your change is like desiring to live in a warm house during winter time, but never cutting on the heater to make it a reality. Nobody died for you to have it that easy, so strap up your boots, get you some good tap water and start your new and improved journey. If you have not finished your GED, if you are afraid to start that business, if you have that manuscript written but have not submitted it because the people around you won't support it, if you keep cheating on your spouse, if you keep disrespecting your husband verbally, if your attitude continues to push people away, or if you're just caught up in the crooked functions of this world, you need to get that change in order to make ends meet. If you can think it, vision it, believe that it's possible, and pursue it, then the universe will release what's already yours. It's not your environment, it's not your kids, it's not your financial situation, it's not your school, it's not your supervisor, and it's not your church building. It's the strength and quality of your mind that predicts your future. This is a blue collar parable for you to be able to tap into what's already yours. You need to no longer be deceived by what you're able to see and hear, as well as what you're unable to see and hear, because of man hiding it from you; it's no longer a secret!!! Peace & Ubuntu, Merv

A Kid with Royal Swag

We oftentimes overlook the testimonies of our youth, and the experiences they encounter. If we allow them to share, lives may me changed. I decided to give this young thirteen year old Queen a chance to display her Royal Swag through writing.---Peace & Ubuntu, Merv

"My Experience"
By: Iesha Aikens

I have learned so many things from my Auntie Sandra Williams Rowe. One thing she always told me is that "you can't always take matters into your own hands, because it may get chaotic." My experience was pretty chaotic indeed. At school in 2013, I got suspended for five days for fighting. The reason I was fighting was because one of my closest friends told me that another girl wanted to fight me. One thing led to another and I took matters into my own hands by fighting. Of course, I received a five day suspension and while home I felt depressed, because I LOVE SCHOOL so much. I couldn't see my friends and I was so bored because I had nothing to do but write 300-500 word essays about my experience, and watch TV. School to me means that I get the chance to show others that I am smart. It also means that I get to show everyone that I don't have to make the same mistakes that my mother

[179]

did. You see, she made some poor decisions in life, and that's why my brother and I have to stay with my Auntie. Hopefully the future will get better for her because I LOVE HER SO MUCH.

The one thing that depressed me the most about missing school was that I messed up my cheerleading privileges and I took pleasure in that. My football cheering was taken away from me until basketball season started, but that was still painful. My suspension taught me a couple of things, such as, you can't always take matters into your own hands, and you have to tell an adult in that kind of situation, even if it takes you looking weak. When I went back to school, I was the happiest girl in the world, but then again, I was the saddest. The reason I was sad was because I knew my family and teachers where disappointed in me, and that everybody was going to be talking about the fight, so I prepared myself for the he say she say stuff. One thing for sure is that I would never handle that situation the same ever again, because I am in charge of my decisions. I was so happy to see my friends again and to be back in a learning environment, that I won't do anything to mess that up again. They can call me a snitch when I tell an adult, but I consider it benefiting me and my future. I gained motivation from the situation that caused me to act out of character, but it won't happen again, because I have royal swag and I stand to say, "Not This One."

Youth: Iesha Aikens
Grade: 7th
Age: 13
School: Madison County Fl. Central School Broncos
Favorite Teacher: Tyesha Fogle
Dream: To become a lawyer

Acknowledgments

It is my honor to first and foremost give thanks to my heavenly Father for providing me with Your Word. I thank my wife, and Queen, Denise, for being that pink rock in my life that held me up when this world is trying to push me down. Every day is not sunny, but you really do make me appreciate marriage, I love you. To my daughter Lyric (first born), daddy loves you so much, and I pray that I have led by example and showed you what to look for in a man, by you watching me, and how I treat your mom. To my little son TJ, daddy loves you, and never forget that. You are going to be a great leader one day. I pray that I have led and am leading by example, so that you will know what being a real man is. Mom and Dad, when I tell you that I am a blessed son to have you, I really mean it. You all have been through so much the past two years and I have only seen growth. To all of my siblings, my in laws, my entire family, my Boyz to Kings Family, my community partners, Katrina Aikens, Rhonda Moore, Craig Wilson, David Dukes, Marcus Hawkins, Preston Matthews, Edna Turner, Cindy Vees, Emily Spencer, Evelyn Turner, Charles Colson, Donna Haggan, Octavious Tookes, Tonya Bell, Kim Barnhill, David Jonas, Deveda Bellamy, Michael Curtis, Ksena Zipperer, Kim Scarboro, Lou Miller, Orlando family, and more. I thank you all so much for keeping it real---Peace & Ubuntu, Merv

"UBUNTU"

"Supporting another individual's dream is genuine when we do it even before our own dreams become a full reality."

Merv Mattair

1. "From Tribulations to Triumph: The Inspirational Story of Tammy Monlyn" **Author**: Desmond J. Roberson Sr. (This is a tear jerker---Merv)
2. "Genesis of a Poetess: Motivational poems" **Author**: Dawn Desiree Banks
3. "Getting Along With You Know Who" **Author**: Reginald E. Daniels
4. "Daybreak: Gaining Strength Through Our Pain: Inspirational poems" **Author**: Angela Y. Hodge
5. "Like Whispers from Heaven: Inspirational poems" **Author**: Carol R. Griffin
6. "Church Folk Can Be Dangerous People" **Author**: Sidney Crudup
7. "I Have Never Lived In America" **Author**: Civil Rights Leader, Mr. David Dukes
8. "Woman to Woman: The Truth About Singleness and Marriage" **Author**: Elaine C. Whittaker

CPSIA information can be obtained at www.ICGtesting.com
Printed in the USA
LVOW13s1434160814

399384LV00001B/82/P